CW00481246

THE ULTIMATE
NINJA DUAL ZONE
AIR FRYER COOKBOOK 2023

1001-Day Super-Easy, Energy-Saving & Delicious Air Fryer Recipes for Beginners and Pros

Copyright©2023 **Andrew Spriggs**
All rights reserved. No part of this book may be reproduced
or used in any manner without the prior written permission
of the copyright owner, except for the use of brief quotations
in a book review.
First paperback edition May 2023.
Printed by Amazon in the USA.
Disclaimer : Although the author and publisher have made every effort to ensure that
the information in this book was correct at press time, the author and publisher do not
assume and hereby disclaim any liability to any party for any loss, damage, or disruption
caused by errors or omissions, whether such errors or omissions result from negligence,
accident, or any other cause. this book is not intended as a substitute for the medical
advice of physicians.

CONTENTS

FISH & SEAFOOD RECIPES 44

BEEF, PORK & LAMB RECIPES 54

INTRODUCTION

An air fryer is a kitchen appliance that allows you to cook foods with hot air instead of oil. It's like having your mini convection oven on your countertop! Air fryers rapidly circulate hot air around the food inside the basket or tray. This creates a crispy exterior while locking in moisture and flavor inside. Unlike deep frying or baking in oil, there's no need for excess oils or fats when using an air fryer, making it a healthier cooking option overall. Using my air fryer has become second nature now that I understand its functionality. With adjustable temperature controls and various settings, including pre-programmed modes for specific foods like chicken wings or French fries – cooking with my air fryer feels effortless and foolproof. Plus, it cooks frozen foods well, and fresh veggies are given a new life thanks to this nifty appliance!

BENEFITS OF USING AN AIR FRYER FOR COOKING CANNED FOODS

HEALTHIER COOKING METHOD

I love using my air fryer for cooking canned foods because it's healthier than deep-frying. Using hot air instead of oil makes the food crispy without adding unnecessary calories and fat. This technique also helps retain more nutrients, making it an excellent option for those who want to eat healthily. I don't have to worry about that greasy feeling after eating fried foods. Air frying canned vegetables like green beans or baked goods like biscuits can be a tasty way to enjoy them without all the added fats from traditional frying methods. For example, when I air fry canned green beans with some seasoning and a touch of oil spray, they come out perfectly crispy on the outside and tender on the inside – just what I'm looking for in a side dish! It's amazing how such simple changes can make our meals healthier while tasting delicious. Overall, using an air fryer as an alternative cooking method is perfect for those who want to cut back on oily or fatty foods but still enjoy satisfying snacks and meals. Learning how to cook canned foods in my air fryer has been fun and rewarding as someone who loves experimenting with different recipes and ingredients.

TIME-SAVING

Using an air fryer to cook canned foods is not only healthier but also a time-saving method.

You can have your favorite canned foods cooked in just minutes with the right temperature and timing settings. Compared to traditional cooking methods such as baking or frying, an air fryer reduces cooking time by about 20-30%. It saves cooking time, and cleanup is faster and easier with an air fryer. Unlike conventional ovens or stovetops that require multiple pots and pans, air fryers typically have one removable basket that's easy to clean. Plus, they don't produce much smoke or odor during cooking, making them ideal for quick meals on busy days.

VERSATILITY IN COOKING DIFFERENT TYPES OF CANNED FOODS

One of the most significant benefits of air frying canned foods is its versatility in cooking different canned foods. You can cook almost anything in a can using an air fryer, from vegetables and meats to baked goods, seafood, snacks, and appetizers. For example, canned green beans are a popular vegetable easily cooked in an air fryer for a healthier alternative to traditional fried green beans.

And if you're looking for something more substantial, try making honey-barbecue chicken wings or spicy tuna cakes using your air fryer. The possibilities are endless when it comes to cooking canned foods in an air fryer. With so many options available, knowing which canned foods work best for air frying and how to prepare them properly before placing them inside the appliance is essential.

With these tips and tricks under your belt, you'll be on your way to creating delicious meals with ease!

REDUCED OIL USAGE

One of the most significant benefits of cooking canned foods in an air fryer is the reduced use of oil. Unlike traditional frying methods, you only need a fraction of the oil to achieve crispy and delicious results. This makes it a healthier alternative for those conscious of their calorie intake.

With less oil usage, air frying also minimizes the risk of ingesting harmful substances in heated oils. Compared to deep-frying or sautéing, air frying allows you to cook your favorite canned foods with minimal added fats without compromising taste and texture. By choosing the suitable types of canned foods and coating them lightly with seasoning or batter, you'll have a guilt-free pleasure that will satisfy your cravings without sacrificing your health goals.

CHOOSING THE BEST CANNED FOODS FOR AIR FRYING

When choosing canned foods to air fry, consider the types of vegetables, meats, baked goods, seafood, and snacks that can be fried with reduced oil usage and increased crispiness.

VEGETABLES---I love air frying vegetables because they are healthier and deliver crispy and delicious results. My favorite canned vegetables to cook in the air fryer are green beans and corn, but you can use almost any vegetable you have on hand. Just remember to drain excess liquid before coating them with seasoning or batter. One crucial tip for air frying veggies is not to overcrowd the basket. This ensures that each piece gets evenly cooked and crispy. I also recommend setting the temperature between 375-400°F and cooking for 8-12 minutes, depending on your desired level of crispiness. And if you want an added flavor, try tossing your veggies in a bit of melted butter or oil mixed with herbs or spices before adding them to the basket!

MEATS---Meats can be a delicious addition to your air fryer repertoire. Some great canned meat options include chicken, beef, and pork. Before cooking, drain any excess liquid from the can and pat dry with paper towels. When preparing canned meats for air frying, you can coat them in various seasonings or batter for added flavor and texture. Remember that wet batter should be avoided as it will not cook evenly in the air fryer. Instead, use a dry coating or spices like paprika or garlic powder. By following these tips and experimenting with different recipes, you'll soon discover how versatile your air fryer can be when cooking canned meats!

BAKED GOODS---Baked goods are a delicious addition to any meal and can be made even better using an air fryer. Canned biscuits, cinnamon rolls, and gingerbread bites are just a few examples of baked goods that can be made in the air fryer. The reduced oil usage makes them healthier and creates a crispy outer layer. When preparing canned baked goods for air frying, it's important to coat them with seasoning or batter before cooking. This will help enhance their flavor and create an even crispier texture. Wet batter foods should not be placed in the air fryer since they tend to cook unevenly, while corn dogs should be pre-fried before being air fried for best results. Following these tips and tricks, you can enjoy perfectly cooked canned baked goods straight from your trusty air fryer!

SEAFOOD---I love cooking seafood in my air fryer. It's a healthier alternative to deep frying and cooks the fish to a perfect crisp. My favorite canned seafood to air fry include shrimp, crab cakes, and even tuna patties. Before you air fry your seafood, drain any excess liquid from the can and season it with your preferred spices or batter for extra flavor. Set your air fryer temperature between 350-400 degrees Fahrenheit, depending on the type of fish you're cooking, and cook them for about 5-8 minutes per side until they are crispy on the outside and tender on the inside. Remember not to overcrowd your air fryer basket, which can cause uneven cooking or lead to food sticking together. With these simple tips, you'll be able to enjoy perfectly cooked canned seafood every time!

SNACKS AND APPETIZERS---Don't forget about snacks and appetizers when it comes to air-frying canned foods. Air fryers can create deliciously crispy and healthier versions of favorite crunchy snacks like popcorn or kale chips.For a heartier snack or party appetizer, try air-frying frozen meatballs or chicken wings for a quick cook time and crispy texture. Remember that wet batter foods should be avoided in the air fryer, but a light coating of seasoning or breadcrumbs can add extra flavor to your snack creations. Another great option for snacking is air-fried sweet potato fries. Sweet potatoes are an excellent source of vitamins A and C and are perfect for those seeking a healthier alternative to traditional french fries. Slice the sweet potatoes into thin strips, coat them with oil and seasoning, then pop them into the air fryer until crispy and tender. With these tasty options, your next game-day spread will be a hit!

PREPARING CANNED FOODS FOR AIR FRYING

Before air frying canned foods, it's essential to drain excess liquid from them and coat them with seasoning or batter for added flavor and texture.

Draining Excess Liquid

When preparing canned foods for air frying, one essential step is draining excess liquid. This is because too much liquid can cause steam, making your food come out soggy instead of crispy.
Ensure you use a strainer or colander to drain any excess water while shaking it well to prevent dripping. For best results, it's recommended that you pat dry the canned foods with paper towels after draining off any liquids. Doing this helps remove more moisture from the food and provides a dry surface for seasoning or coating with batter. By draining excess liquid before cooking, your air-fried canned foods will come out deliciously crispy and perfectly cooked inside!

Coating With Seasoning Or Batter

When it comes to air frying canned foods, adding seasoning or batter can make a world of difference in taste and texture. Try coating vegetables like green beans or sliced potatoes with breadcrumbs mixed with your favorite spices for crispy results. Mix cinnamon and sugar and dredge slices of canned pineapple before placing them in the air fryer for a sweeter option. However, it's important to note that wet batter should not be used when cooking canned foods in an air fryer. The high heat from the appliance will cause the batter to blow around inside the basket and cook unevenly. Instead, opt for dry coatings like panko breadcrumbs or crushed cornflakes for that perfect crunch without making a mess.

Setting Up Your Air Fryer For Cooking Canned Foods

To ensure your canned foods are cooked to perfection in your air fryer, it's vital to set up the appliance correctly – this includes selecting the right temperature and time settings and preheating the basket. Read on for more tips and tricks on making the most out of your air fryer when cooking canned foods!

Temperature And Time Settings

When it comes to air frying canned foods, setting the right temperature and time is crucial for a successful outcome. It's always best to refer to the manual that came with your air fryer for guidance. Generally, most air fryers have a temperature range between 200-400°F, and cooking times can vary between 5-25 minutes depending on your cooking. Preheating your air fryer beforehand is also essential, ensuring even cooking and better results. Once preheated, adjust the temperature settings and watch the food cook. It's always helpful to shake or flip your food halfway through cooking time for an evenly cooked result. Remember, every dish has unique temperature requirements, so consult recipe instructions before starting.

Preheating The Air Fryer

Preheating your air fryer ensures that your canned foods cook evenly and crisp. To preheat your air fryer, set the temperature to the recommended level and allow it to heat up for a few minutes before adding your food. It's important not to overcrowd the basket during this process as it can affect the cooking time. Once preheated, place your canned foods in the basket and set the timer according to the recipe or instructions on the packaging. Remember to check on your food halfway through cooking, using tongs or a spatula to flip them over for even cooking. By taking these steps and following our helpful tips, you'll be able to achieve deliciously crispy canned foods cooked in an air fryer every time!

CLEANING YOUR AIR FRYER PROPERLY

Cleaning your air fryer properly is crucial to maintaining its efficiency and prolonging lifespan.
This includes removing excess grease and food debris, wiping down the interior and exterior of the appliance, as well as checking and replacing the air filter regularly.

Removing excess grease and food debris

I always make sure to clean my air fryer properly after each use. To remove excess grease and food debris, I use a damp cloth or sponge to wipe down the exterior and interior of the appliance. It's important to be gentle while cleaning to not damage the non-stick coating. Another helpful tip is removing leftover crumbs or debris from the bottom of the basket using a kitchen brush or toothbrush. Add dish soap and water to your cloth or sponge for extra cleaning power if there are stubborn stains. Keeping your air fryer clean and free from buildup will perform better and last longer overall.

Wiping Down the Interior And Exterior Of The Air Fryer

Keeping your air fryer clean is essential to prevent buildup and ensure optimal performance. Wiping down the interior and exterior of the air fryer is crucial in maintaining its longevity. After each use, allow the appliance to cool before unplugging it and wiping down the inside with a damp cloth. To clean the exterior of your air fryer, wipe it down with a damp cloth or sponge. Avoid using harsh chemicals or abrasive materials that could damage the surface. Regular cleaning will keep your appliance looking new and prevent any unwanted odors from forming while cooking different types of foods. Remember to also check and replace your air filter regularly per manufacturer instructions. This ensures that airflow remains consistent during cooking, resulting in evenly cooked food every time you prepare something delicious in your beloved air fryer!

Checking And Replacing The Air Filter Regularly

A critical aspect of maintaining your air fryer is regularly checking and replacing the air filter. The air filter ensures that your appliance operates properly by preventing dust and other particles from entering the heating element. Over time, the air filter can become dirty, clogged, or damaged, affecting its ability to trap debris effectively. To check the condition of your air filter, gently remove it from its slot at the back of the unit. If you notice any signs of damage or excessive buildup on the filter, it's time to replace it with a new one. Most manufacturers recommend replacing your air filter every three months for optimal performance and longevity of your appliance. By checking and replacing your air filters regularly, you'll enjoy better-tasting foods cooked in a cleaner environment while extending the lifespan of your valuable kitchen gadget.

AIR FRYERS FREQUENTLY ASKED QUESTIONS

Can I put oil in an air fryer? ----- Most recipes only call for about 1 tablespoon of oil, which is best applied with a mister. Fatty foods, like bacon, won't need you to add any oil. Leaner meats, however, will need some oiling to keep them from sticking to the pan.

What shouldn't you put in an Air Fryer? ----- The Air Fryer is one of those kitchen inventions that seem too good to be true. You can cook practically any food in the hot air multi-cooker. However, there are mistakes a lot of us do when handling an air fryer including not preheating your air fryer, not giving the air fryer enough space, overcrowding the air fryer basket, using too little oil, cutting vegetables too small, using wet batters and not washing the air fryer often enough.

Can I use Aluminum Foil or Baking Paper in the Air Fryer? ----- As a general rule, you can use both on the bottom of the air fryer if the basket sits on top. Using aluminum foil or baking paper in the basket technically can be done as long as it's weighed down by the food however it's not recommended because an air fryer works by providing a constant air flow around the cooking cavity.

Should I shake the basket while cooking? ----- Yes, shaking is allowed. A number of foods will stick to the basket if you don't shake it while cooking. Giving it a little shake is specially helpful if you overlap foods, this way the contents of the basket will cook evenly.

What's the first thing I should cook in my new Air Fryer? ----- The most common foods to start with are French Fries, and also Chicken Drumsticks.

What are the disadvantages to cooking in an Air Fryer? ----- The only real disadvantage to cooking in an air fryer is the fact most of the air fryers on the market have small cooking cavities.

What kind of foods can you cook in an Air Fryer? ----- The air fryer is your ticket to healthier fried foods that still taste crispy-crunchy delicious and leaves you with a lot less mess at clean-up time. Whether frozen food or raw meat or reheating leftover food, the hot air multi-cooker does a fantastic job. Having an air fryer means you can go ahead and cook frozen food such as frozen fries, nuggets, fish sticks etc. You can also cook raw meat, for example you can roast chicken or pork in the fryer. And you can certainly roast vegetables and nuts too and let's not forget you can easily bake small items.

Should I pause the Air Fryer when checking on the food? ----- Since you generally only spend a matter of seconds checking, or shaking the food, it is not necessary to pause the air fryer.

Can I open the Air Fryer while cooking? ----- Every Air Fryer is slightly different however going on the premise that heat rises, if your air fryer opens by sliding a basket out from the side or front, then there should be no reason why you can't open the basket for short periods of time.

Should I preheat the Air Fryer? ----- Every Air Fryer manufacturer will have their own recommendations for their particular air fryer. This is also a good idea since many users find that cooking times are more accurate if you preheat first.

Why are my cooking times different? -----Not all Air Fryers are created equal. Air Fryers work by circulating hot air around the food. The internal shape of the Air Fryer and how the air flows, as well as how hot the air is all contribute to how long it takes to cook a food. This is why you should check often and only use temperatures as a guide until you know how your particular Air Fryer cooks.

What are the advantages to cooking in an Air Fryer? ----- Advantages are many, like we said before, we're talking about a healthier form of cooking. Even though your food is fried it won't be dripping with oil. It's less expensive to run. Cooking in an air fryer is very quick. Also, food cooked in an air fryer is generally really tasty simply because the food is crispy on the outside, and juicy and tender on the inside.

BREAKFAST & BRUNCH RECIPES

Air Fryer German Pancake Bites

Ingredients:
- Pancakes:
- 6 eggs
- 1 cup whole milk
- 1 tsp salt
- 1 cup all-purpose flour
- Toppings Options:
- Chocolate hazelnut spread
- Berries
- Banana slices

Directions:
1. In a large bowl, beat together eggs and milk. Sift in flour and salt. MIx well with electric mixer and set aside.
2. Lightly butter ramekins or 4 small oven-safe cups. Fill each container 1/4 full of batter.
3. Place in air fryer and set to 400F for 6 minutes.
4. Carefully remove pancake bites from ramekins and top with your favorite toppings!
5. Enjoy!

Air Fryer "pretzel" Bites & Irish Pub Beer Cheese

Servings: 6

Ingredients:
- Pretzel Bites:
- 1 can prepared biscuits
- 8 cups water
- ⅓ cup baking soda
- ¼ cup butter, melted
- 2 tablespoons flaky salt or pretzel salt
- Items Needed:
- Slotted spoon
- Food processor fitted with blade attachment
- Small heatproof baking dish
- Beer Cheese:
- 6 ounces cream cheese
- 1 cup sharp cheddar cheese, freshly shredded
- 1 cup Irish cheddar cheese, freshly shredded
- 1 cup Fontina cheese, freshly shredded
- ⅔ cup stout beer
- 3 garlic cloves, minced
- 1 tablespoon spicy brown mustard
- 1½ teaspoons Worcestershire sauce
- 1 teaspoon paprika
- 1 teaspoon kosher salt
- 1 tablespoon fresh chives, chopped, for garnish

Directions:
1. Cut the individual biscuits into quarters and roll into balls. Set aside.
2. Bring the water to a boil in a large saucepan and add the baking soda. Boil the biscuit dough balls for 15 to 20 seconds at a time, then transfer to a tray using a slotted spoon.
3. Place the crisper plate into the Smart Air Fryer basket, then place the boiled dough balls onto the crisper plate in a single layer.
4. Brush the dough balls with melted butter and sprinkle with flaky salt or pretzel salt.
5. Select the Air Fry function, adjust time to 10 minutes, then press Start/Pause. Open the basket to brush the pretzel bites with butter every 3 to 4 minutes.
6. Remove the pretzel bites when done.
7. Place the cream cheese and all three shredded cheeses into the bowl of a food processor fitted with the blade attachment. Blend until fully combined.
8. Add the beer, garlic, mustard, Worcestershire sauce, paprika, and salt into the food processor and blend until smooth.
9. Transfer the cheese into a small heatproof baking dish.
10. Place the baking dish onto the crisper plate.
11. Select the Broil function, adjust time to 5 minutes, then press Start/Pause.
12. Remove the beer cheese when done, garnish with chives, and serve with the pretzel bites.

Air Fryer Cinnamon Rolls

Servings: 4
Cooking Time: 20 Minutes

Ingredients:
- 1 ounce cream cheese
- 1 tablespoon unsalted butter
- All-purpose flour
- 1 (8-ounce) tube refrigerated crescent roll dough
- 1/4 cup packed light brown sugar
- 1 1/2 teaspoons ground cinnamon
- 1/4 cup powdered sugar
- 1 tablespoon whole or 2% milk

Directions:
1. Cut 1 ounce cream cheese into 8 pieces. Place in a medium bowl and let sit at room temperature to soften while you prepare the cinnamon rolls.
2. Place 1 tablespoon unsalted butter in a small microwave-safe bowl and microwave until melted, about 30 seconds. (Alternatively, melt the butter on the stovetop in a small saucepan.) Let cool slightly. Meanwhile, heat an air fryer to 325°F.
3. Add 1/4 cup packed light brown sugar and 1 1/2 teaspoons ground cinnamon to the butter and stir to combine.
4. Cut a sheet of parchment paper about the size of the air fryer basket or tray and place on a work surface. Unroll 1 tube crescent roll dough onto the parchment. Gently press the seams together with your fingers. (It doesn't have to be perfect.) Spread the cinnamon-sugar mixture evenly onto the dough, leaving a 1/2-inch border. Gently press into the dough. Starting at a long side, tightly roll up the dough. Use your fingers to tightly press and seal the seam. Arrange seam-side down and cut crosswise into 8 pieces.
5. Arrange the rolls cut-side up, touching on another, on the parchment paper. Slide, still on the parchment, into the air fryer basket or onto the tray. Air fry until puffed and golden brown, 20 minutes. Let cool on the tray or in the basket for 5 minutes. Meanwhile, make the icing.
6. Add 1/4 cup powdered sugar to the cream cheese. Stir until smooth. Whisk in 1 tablespoon milk until thinned and smooth. Spread over the warm rolls and serve immediately.

RECIPE NOTES
Storage: Leftovers can be wrapped in plastic wrap and refrigerated for up to 1 week. Rewarm in a 300°F oven until warmed through, about 10 minutes.

Air Fryer Nutella French Toast Roll-ups

Servings: 4
Cooking Time: 6 Minutes

Ingredients:
- 10 slices of bread
- 3 large eggs
- 2 tbsp milk
- 4 tbsp granulated white sugar
- 1 tsp cinnamon
- 10 tsp Nutella

Directions:
1. If you haven't already, lay the bread out for 30 minutes to an hour to allow it to become stale.
2. If you're planning ahead, you can leave the bread out over night.
3. Whisk together the eggs and milk and set aside.
4. In a small dish, mix the cinnamon and sugar and set aside.
5. Cut the crust off of the slices of bread and then take a glass or rolling pin to flatten the bread.
6. Take a teaspoon of Nutella and spread on one end of the flattened bread. Roll the bread up, and dab a little Nutella on the end to help keep the rolls closed and secure during cooking.
7. Dip the french toast roll-ups in the egg mixture and then roll into the cinnamon and sugar mixture.
8. Place the Nutella French Toast Rolls ups into the prepared air fryer basket. Cook on 360 degrees Fahrenheit for 5-6 minutes, flipping the roll-ups halfway through.

9. Serve immediately.
NOTES
You can use just about anything if you don't have Nutella. Strawberries, blueberries, apples, peanut butter and jelly, or just skip the filling and leave them plain. Either way, they are delicious!

Air Fryer Ham And Swiss Crescent Rolls
Servings: 4

Ingredients:
- 1 can (8 oz) refrigerated Pillsbury™ Original Crescent Rolls (8 Count)
- 8 thin slices deli ham (3.5 oz)
- 4 thin slices Swiss cheese (3 oz), each cut into 4 strips

Directions:
1. Cut 8-inch round of cooking parchment paper; place in bottom of air fryer basket.
2. Unroll dough; separate into 8 triangles. Place 1 piece of ham on each triangle; place 2 strips of cheese down center of ham. Fold in edges of ham to match shape of dough triangle. Roll up each crescent, ending at tip of triangle.
3. On parchment paper in air fryer basket, place 4 crescent rolls point sides down. Cover remaining crescent rolls with plastic wrap, and refrigerate.
4. Set air fryer to 300°F; cook 6 minutes. With tongs, turn over each one; cook 4 to 7 minutes longer or until golden brown. Remove from air fryer. Repeat with remaining 4 crescent rolls. Serve warm.

Air Fryer French Toast Sticks
Servings: 4
Cooking Time: 10 Minutes

Ingredients:
- 5 slices of bread
- 2 eggs
- 1/3 cup milk
- 3 tablespoons sugar
- 2 tablespoons flour
- 1 teaspoon ground cinnamon
- 1/2 teaspoon vanilla extract
- 1/8 teaspoon salt
- OPTIONAL
- Confectioners sugar for dusting
- Maple syrup for dipping

Directions:
1. Preheat your air fryer to 370 degrees.
2. Cut each piece of bread into 3 equal pieces and set aside.
3. Put the eggs, milk, flour, sugar, vanilla, ground cinnamon, and salt into a wide shallow dish. Whisk to combine.
4. Dip each piece of bread into the egg mixture, making sure to coat on all sides.
5. Place a piece of parchment round paper inside the air fryer and place each french toast stick in one single layer on top of the parchment round (needed to prevent sticking).
6. Cook for about 10 minutes, flipping halfway through.
7. Carefully remove the air fryer french toast sticks from the air fryer and enjoy immediately, store in the fridge for up to 3 days, or freeze up to 3 months.
NOTES
HOW TO REHEAT FRENCH TOAST STICKS IN THE AIR FRYER:
Preheat your air fryer to 350 degrees.
Cook french toast sticks for 2-3 minutes until warmed and enjoy!
HOW TO COOK FROZEN FRENCH TOAST STICKS IN THE AIR FRYER:
Preheat your air fryer to 320 degrees.
Cook frozen french toast sticks in the air fryer for 2-3 minutes until warmed and enjoy!

Breakfast Oat Cake
Servings: 1
Cooking Time: 15 Minutes

Ingredients:
- 1/2 banana
- 1/2 cup rolled oats
- 1/3 cup milk of choice
- 1/2 tsp bp
- 1/4 tsp flaked sea salt
- 1T honey
- 1 egg

- 1 square dark chocolate, diced
- 1 Tbsp Cacao (optional for a chocolate cookie cake)
- Vegan Adaption: increase the milk to ⅔ cup, replace the egg with 1Tbsp chia soaked with 2 ½ Tbsp water

Directions:
1. Place the oats, banana, milk, baking powder, salt, oats, and honey in a blender. Blend for 1 minute on high until well combined and the oats are a fine puree.
2. Heat the Instant Vortex to Bake at a temperature of 177C for 13 minutes.
3. Pour the oats into a 250ml ramekin, then place in the preheated Instant Vortex.
4. Once golden brown and cooked through, remove from the Vortex and serve immediately.

Air Fryer Eggplant Parmesan
Servings: 4
Cooking Time: 20 Minutes

Ingredients:
- ½ cup Italian bread crumbs
- ¼ cup freshly grated Parmesan cheese
- 1 teaspoon Italian seasoning
- 1 teaspoon salt
- ½ teaspoon dried basil
- ½ teaspoon garlic powder
- ½ teaspoon onion powder
- ½ teaspoon freshly ground black pepper
- ¼ cup flour
- 2 large eggs, beaten
- 1 medium eggplant, sliced into 1/2-inch rounds
- 1 cup marinara sauce, or more to taste
- 8 slices mozzarella cheese, or as needed

Directions:
1. Combine bread crumbs, Parmesan cheese, Italian seasoning, salt, basil, garlic powder, onion powder, and black pepper in a shallow bowl. Place flour in a separate shallow bowl and beaten eggs in a third shallow bowl.
2. Dip sliced eggplant first in flour, then in beaten eggs, and finally coat with bread crumb mixture. Place coated eggplant on a tray and let rest for 5 minutes.
3. Preheat an air fryer to 370 degrees F (185 degrees C).
4. Place breaded eggplant rounds in the air fryer basket, making sure they are not touching; work in batches if necessary. Cook for 8 to 10 minutes, flip each round, and cook until desired crispiness is achieved, 4 to 6 minutes more.
5. Top each eggplant round with marinara sauce and 1 slice of mozzarella cheese. Place the basket back in the air fryer and cook until cheese has started to melt, 1 to 2 minutes. Repeat with remaining eggplant, if necessary.
6. Serve hot and enjoy!

Air Fryer Lasagna Egg Rolls
Servings: 15
Cooking Time: 30 Minutes

Ingredients:
- 3 cups (710 ml) cooked lasagna , cooled
- 1 cup (112 g) shredded mozzarella cheese
- 15 (15) egg roll wrappers
- water , for sealing the wrappers
- oil spray , for coating the egg rolls
- 1/2-1 cup (120-240 ml) dipping sauce of choice , marinara, ranch, bbq sauce, etc.
- EQUIPMENT
- Air Fryer

Directions:
1. Cook the lasagna and then let cool to at least room temperature or use leftover lasagna. Cut into small slices about 2 Tablespoons in volume.
2. Using egg roll wrappers or spring roll wrappers, add the 2 Tablespoons piece of the lasagna filling to each wrapper. Add about 2 teaspoons of shredded cheese on top. Tuck and roll the wrapper around the filling (watch the video in the post above to see how to roll even and tight rolls). Brush the top corner of the wrapper with water to help seal the wrapper end, and then finish rolling the egg roll. Repeat for all the egg rolls.

3. Brush or spray rolls with oil to coat. Place egg rolls in a single layer in the air fryer basket (cook in batches).
4. Air Fry 380°F for 12-16 minutes, flipping halfway through. Cook until the wrapper is crispy and browned. If you use the larger wrapper or if your wrappers are thicker cook a little longer so that all the layers can cook through to avoid being tough and chewy.
5. Allow to cool a little (the filling will be super hot right after cooking), and then serve with your favorite dipping sauce.

Air Fryer Frozen Hash Brown Patties

Servings: 4
Cooking Time: 15 Minutes

Ingredients:
- 4 Frozen Hash Brown Patties
- salt , optional to taste
- black pepper , optional to taste
- EQUIPMENT
- Air Fryer

Directions:
1. Place the frozen hash brown patties in the air fryer basket and spread in an even layer (make sure they aren't overlapping). No oil spray is needed.
2. Air Fry at 380°F/193°C for 10 minutes. Flip the hashbrown patties over.
3. Continue to Air Fry at 380°F/193°C for an additional 2-5 minutes or until crisped to your liking. Season with salt & pepper, if desired.

NOTES
Air Frying Tips and Notes:
No Oil Necessary. Cook Frozen - Do not thaw first.
Turn as needed. Cook in a single layer in the air fryer basket.
Recipe timing is based on a non-preheated air fryer. If cooking in multiple batches back to back, the following batches may cook a little quicker.

Recipes were tested in 3.7 to 6 qt. air fryers. If using a larger air fryer, the hash browns might cook quicker so adjust cooking time.
Remember to set a timer to flip as directed in recipe.

Air Fryer Brisket Tacos

Servings: 4
Cooking Time: 12 Minutes

Ingredients:
- 8 small corn tortillas
- 2 cups leftover beef brisket
- ¼ cup red onions diced
- 1 avocado diced
- 1 lime juiced
- 2 tablespoons cilantro chopped
- toppings as desired for serving

Directions:
1. Preheat the air fryer to 400°F.
2. Wrap the tortillas in foil and place in the air fryer for 3-4 minutes or until warmed. Remove from the air fryer and set aside.
3. While the tortillas are warming, combine avocado, red onion, lime, and cilantro in a bowl. Season with salt an set aside.
4. Chop or pull the brisket into pieces and place in the air fryer. Cook 3-5 minutes or until heated through and it begins to crisp.
5. Top each tortilla with ¼ cup of brisket and a spoonful of the salsa mixture.
6. Drizzle with sour cream and a sprinkle of cheese if desired.

Air Fryer Egg Rolls

Servings: 4 - 6

Ingredients:
- 1 tbsp. sesame oil
- 1/2 lb. ground pork
- 4 c. coleslaw mix
- 1/2 c. matchstick-cut carrots
- 1 tsp. freshly grated ginger
- 2 garlic cloves, minced
- 3 green onions, sliced
- 2 tsp. soy sauce
- 2 tsp. rice vinegar

- 1/2 tsp. ground black pepper
- 1/4 tsp. kosher salt
- 1/8 tsp. Chinese 5-spice seasoning
- 12 egg roll wrappers
- Nonstick cooking spray
- 1 tbsp. olive oil
- Sweet chili sauce, duck sauce, or hot mustard sauce, for dipping

Directions:
1. Heat the sesame oil in a large skillet over medium heat. Add the pork and cook until crumbled and cooked through, about 4 minutes. Add the coleslaw mix, carrots, ginger and garlic. Cook 2-3 minutes or until the cabbage has wilted. Remove from the heat; stir in the green onions, soy sauce, vinegar, pepper, salt, and 5-spice seasoning. Transfer to a plate and let cool slightly.
2. Place 1 egg roll wrapper on a dry work surface with the points of the wrapper facing up and down (like a diamond). Place about 1/3 cup of the pork mixture in the middle of the wrapper. Dip your fingers in water and and dampen the edges of the wrapper. Fold the left then right points of the wrapper in toward the center. Fold the bottom point over the center. Roll toward the remaining point to form a tight cylinder. Press edges to seal. Place on a plate and cover with a dry towel. Repeat the process with remaining wrappers and pork mixture.
3. Preheat the air fryer to 360°, if required. Spray the air fryer basket with cooking spray. Brush the tops of the egg rolls with olive oil. Working in 3 batches (4 at a time), place the egg rolls in the basket and cook 7 minutes. Flip the egg rolls over and brush with more oil. Cook for an additional 2 minutes.
4. Serve with the dipping sauce of your choice.
Notes
If you have ginger paste in your refrigerator, use 2 teaspoons in place of the 1 teaspoon of freshly grated ginger.

Air Fryer Baked Oats
Ingredients:
- 1 cup oats
- 1/2cup milk of choice
- 1 tablespoon lemon curd flavoured yogurt
- 1 teaspoon baking powder
- 1 banana
- 1 flat teaspoon cinnamon
- 2 teaspoon honey
- 5/6 raspberries
- Dark choc chips

Directions:
1. In a blender blend all your ingredients besides the raspberries and choc chips. Until it's a smooth paste. Pour into ramekins. Top with raspberries and choc chips. Place into your Vortex air fryer to bake on 160 degrees Celsius for 10 minutes then turn to 180 for 2 more minutes.
2. I added a dollop of lemon curd yogurt to the top. This feels like a dessert or baked pudding for breakfast. You can use any variety of toppings and additions, you could use plain yoghurt I just love the combination of raspberries and lemon.

Air Fried Peanut Butter Cups
Servings: 8
Cooking Time: 5 Minutes
Ingredients:
- 8 Reese's Peanut Butter Cups
- 1 can Refrigerated Crescent Rolls 8 rolls

Directions:
1. To make this recipe, begin by unrolling crescent dough and separating each crescent roll.
2. Place one peanut butter cup at the end of the crescent roll and roll until it is completely wrapped. Be sure to pinch dough to cover and seal any exposed parts of the chocolate.
3. Spray Air Fryer basket with nonstick cooking spray, or line with Air Fryer parchment paper. Place wrapped peanut butter cups in the prepared basket, leaving a small space between each pastry.

4. Air fry at 350 degrees for about 5-7 minutes, until crescent rolls are golden brown.
5. Carefully remove them from the Air Fryer. Dust tops with powdered sugar, drizzle with chocolate syrup or frosting glaze.

NOTES

I make these in my Cosori 5.8 Air Fryer. Depending on the size and wattage of the Air Fryer, you may need to add 1-2 additional minutes to cook time.

Leave enough room between each pastry, allowing room for the roll to puff as it cooks.

Do not stack or overlap in the basket. The dough may not cook evenly.

You can make 4 or 8 in a batch, depending on what will fit in your basket.

Air Fryer Bacon And Egg Breakfast Biscuit Bombs

Servings: 10

Ingredients:
- Biscuit Bombs
- 4 slices bacon, cut into 1/2-inch pieces
- 1 tablespoon butter
- 2 eggs, beaten
- 1/4 teaspoon pepper
- 1 can (10.2 oz) refrigerated Pillsbury™ Grands!™ Southern Homestyle Buttermilk Biscuits (5 Count)
- 2 oz sharp cheddar cheese, cut into ten 3/4-inch cubes
- Egg Wash
- 1 egg
- 1 tablespoon water

Directions:
1. Cut two 8-inch rounds of cooking parchment paper. Place one round in bottom of air fryer basket. Spray with cooking spray.
2. In 10-inch nonstick skillet, cook bacon over medium-high heat until crisp. Remove from pan; place on paper towel. Carefully wipe skillet with paper towel. Add butter to skillet; melt over medium heat. Add 2 beaten eggs and pepper to skillet; cook until eggs are thickened but still moist, stirring frequently. Remove from heat; stir in bacon. Cool 5 minutes.
3. Meanwhile, separate dough into 5 biscuits; separate each biscuit into 2 layers. Press each into 4-inch round. Spoon 1 heaping tablespoonful egg mixture onto center of each round. Top with one piece of the cheese. Gently fold edges up and over filling; pinch to seal. In small bowl, beat remaining egg and water. Brush biscuits on all sides with egg wash.
4. Place 5 of the biscuit bombs, seam sides down, on parchment in air fryer basket. Spray both sides of second parchment round with cooking spray. Top biscuit bombs in basket with second parchment round, then top with remaining 5 biscuit bombs.
5. Set to 325°F; cook 8 minutes. Remove top parchment round; using tongs, carefully turn biscuits, and place in basket in single layer. Cook 4 to 6 minutes longer or until cooked through (at least 165°F).

Air Fryer Avocado Eggs

Servings: 2
Cooking Time: 8 Minutes

Ingredients:
- 2 avocados
- 4 eggs
- salt and pepper to taste
- toppings optional: Salsa, Shredded Cheese, Crumbled Bacon, Hot Sauce

Directions:
1. Line the air fryer basket with parchment paper and set aside.
2. Slice avocado in half, lengthwise, and then carefully remove the pit.
3. Using a spoon, gently remove some of the avocado meat, forming a well where the pit was. Save the removed avocado to top the egg, or to eat separately.
4. Place halves in the air fryer basket, and then carefully crack eggs, breaking direction into each half of the avocado.
5. Air fry at 400 degrees F for 8-12 minutes, depending on how well done you prefer your eggs.
6. Season as desired.

NOTES

Variations

Make an avocado toast - If you want to spread the cooked cream avocado on toast and add a bit of Bagel seasoning, you can create an avocado mixture on bread in no time at all. Simple ingredients can easily make all sorts of an easy breakfast.

Add feta cheese - Putting feta cheese on top of the fried egg sounds awesome. This is a simple way that you can make air fryer-baked eggs with an avocado half taste different easily.

Make it spicy - Add some sweet chili sauce to the top of avocado eggs for a spicy hot flavor combination. You can skip the sweet and add red pepper flakes as well.

Pair with other breakfast foods - Make it a large meal by adding some hash browns, turkey bacon, or even fresh fruit.

Air Fryer Hash Brown Egg Bites

Servings: 7

Ingredients:
- Deselect All
- Nonstick cooking spray, for the mold
- 4 large eggs
- 1/4 cup heavy cream
- Kosher salt
- 2/3 cup shredded Cheddar
- 1/4 cup diced red bell peppers
- 1 scallion, white and green parts sliced
- 1/2 cup shredded frozen hash browns, thawed

Directions:
1. Special equipment: a 7-cavity silicone egg bites mold, 6-quart air fryer
2. Spray the cavities of a 7-cavity silicone egg bites mold with nonstick spray. Whisk together the eggs, heavy cream and 1/2 teaspoon salt in a large glass measuring cup until no white streaks remain.
3. Divide the egg mixture, 1/3 cup of the Cheddar, the bell peppers and scallions among the cavities of the mold. Gently stir the mixture in each cavity with a spoon. Transfer the mold to the basket of a 6-quart air fryer, set it to 300°F and cook for 3 minutes.

4. Meanwhile, combine the hash browns and remaining 1/3 cup Cheddar in a small bowl. Gently top each egg bite with the hash brown-cheese mixture.
5. Set the air fryer to 300°F and cook for 12 minutes more. The top of each bite should be golden brown and the eggs should be set. Remove the mold and let stand for 10 minutes before popping out the egg bites. Serve warm.

Air Fryer Breakfast Burritos

Servings: 4
Cooking Time: 6 Minutes

Ingredients:
- 4 eggs
- ¼ cup milk
- ½ teaspoon chili powder
- ¼ teaspoon salt
- ⅛ tablespoon black pepper
- 4 10 inch flour tortillas
- ½ cup shredded cheddar or Colby and Monterey Jack cheese (2 oz.)
- 1 avocado, halved, seeded, peeled, and chopped
- Olive oil or nonstick cooking spray
- Salsa and/or guacamole (optional)

Directions:
1. Preheat air fryer at 400°F. In a 1-qt. casserole or other oven-going dish whisk together eggs, milk, chili powder, salt, and pepper. Place casserole in air-fryer basket. Cook 6 to 8 minutes or until eggs are set, stirring twice. (If air fryer is smaller, divide egg mixture among 10-oz. ramekins and cook in batches.)
2. Divide egg mixture among tortillas. Sprinkle with cheese and top with avocado. Fold in opposite sides and roll up tortillas. Lightly coat burritos with olive oil or cooking spray. Working in batches if needed, arrange burritos in air-fryer basket. Cook 2 to 3 minutes or until toasted. If desired, serve with salsa and/or guacamole.

Tips

After rolling up tortillas, wrap in plastic wrap. Arrange in an airtight container and freeze up to 3 months. To reheat in the air fryer, preheat air fryer to 375°F. Unwrap burritos and arrange in air fryer basket, seam side down. Lightly coat with olive oil or cooking spray. Air fry for 18 minutes or until browned and heated through, turning once halfway through cooking.

Air Fried Easy Breakfast Pastries
Servings: 4
Cooking Time: 15 Minutes

Ingredients:
- 2 packages refrigerated pie crusts
- A variety of jam, in any flavor you like
- 1 egg, beaten with 1 teaspoon of water
- Icing
- 1/2 cup powdered sugar
- 2-3 tablespoons milk
- Sprinkles

Directions:
1. Roll out the pie dough to about ¼ inch thick. Cut the dough into 6 rectangles about 4" x 6". Spread 2 tablespoons of jam on one side of the rectangle leaving about ½ inch around the edge.
2. Using a pastry brush, coat the edges of the pie dough with egg wash. Add a second pastry rectangle on top and press the edges with a fork. Cut two slits in the top of the dough to vent.
3. Brush the top with egg wash, place on dark-coated, parchment-lined baking sheet.
4. Air Fry at 350°F for 5 minutes, carefully flip the pastries, cook 5 more minutes
5. Carefully move baked pastries to a cooling rack.
6. While the pastries are cooling, make the icing. Combine the powdered sugar and milk until you get the desired consistency. Spread on top of cooled pastries and decorate with sprinkles if desired.

Air Fryer Zucchini Pizza Bites
Servings: 4
Cooking Time: 10 Minutes

Ingredients:
- 2 zucchini (medium sized)

- ¾ cup Primal Kitchen's Roasted Garlic Marinara Sauce
- ¾ cup shredded mozzarella cheese
- ½ cup turkey pepperoni
- 1 tbsp olive oil (for spraying)

Directions:
1. Slice the zucchini into slices that are about ¼ inch thick.
2. Lay the zucchini slices flat in the air fryer basket. Do not overcrowd. The zucchini should not overlap. You will need to do this in batches. Spray the slices with olive oil and cook for 3-4 minutes at 400 degrees F.
3. Add the marinara sauce, shredded mozzarella cheese and turkey pepperoni on top of each zucchini slice.
4. Place the basket back into the air fryer and cook for 4-6 minutes at 400 degrees F or until the cheese melts.
5. Repeat as many times as needed depending on the size of your air fryer. As you are making them, let them cool on a wire cooling rack.

Air Fryer Garlic Bread
Servings: 4
Cooking Time: 6 Minutes

Ingredients:
- Half loaf of bread
- 3 tablespoons butter, softened
- 3 garlic cloves, minced
- 1/2 teaspoon dried Italian seasoning
- small pinch of red pepper flakes

Directions:
1. Preheat your air fryer to 350 degrees.
2. Cut the bread in half or sized to fit your air fryer.
3. Mix the butter, garlic, Italian seasoning, and red pepper flakes in a small bowl.
4. Baste the garlic butter mixture on top of the bread evenly.
5. Place the garlic bread in the air fryer side by side and cook for 6 to 7 minutes until browned to your liking.

DESSERTS RECIPES

Gingerbread Cookies In The Air Fryer

Servings: 12
Cooking Time: 8 Minutes

Ingredients:
- 2 3/4 cups all-purpose flour
- 1 tsp baking soda
- ½ tsp ground cinnamon
- ½ tsp ground nutmeg
- 1/2 tsp ground ginger
- ½ tsp salt
- 1/2 cup butter softened
- 3/4 cup brown sugar
- 1 egg large
- ⅓ cup molasses
- 1 teaspoon vanilla

Directions:
1. In a medium bowl, combine the flour, baking soda, ginger, cinnamon, nutmeg, and salt in a bowl, then set the bowl aside.
2. In a large bowl, or stand mixer, add the butter and sugar. Beat together at medium speed. Add in the egg, vanilla, and molasses. Continue mixing on medium speed until well combined.
3. Slowly, add in the flour mixture, and continue mixing until all ingredients are combined. Scrape the inside of the bowl if needed.
4. Wrap and chill dough for about 30 minutes.
5. On a lightly floured surface, roll the dough about ¼ inch in thickness. Use cookie cutters to cut into your favorite shapes.
6. Place cookies in the air fryer basket, lined with parchment paper.
7. Air fry at 350 degrees F for 8-10 minutes until dough is cooked.
8. Allow cookies to cool for 2-3 minutes before removing from the air fryer basket. Then transfer cookies to a wire rack to cool completely.

NOTES

The great thing about these ginger molasses cookies is that you can use the cookie dough for making fun edible things! Grab some cookie cutters and make shapes besides gingerbread men, or even divide dough so that you can create gingerbread houses as well.

Once you bake cookies, you can decorate the gingerbread people and use royal icing from a pastry bag and create an epic gingerbread man! (or decorate those gingerbread houses!)

Bratapfe With Vanilla Sauce

Servings: 5

Ingredients:
- 45g sultanas (golden raisins)
- 1 tbsp rum or bourbon
- 1/3 cup walnuts, chopped
- 1 tbsp apple jelly
- 1 tbsp honey
- 1/4 tsp ground cinnamon
- Pinch sea salt
- 5 apples, cored
- 1 1/2 tbsp butter, cut in 5 pieces
- 50g confectioners' sugar
- 1 tbsp milk
- 1 tsp vanilla extract

Directions:
1. Place sultanas and rum into a small microwave-safe bowl. Microwave until liquid simmers, about 30 seconds. Set aside.
2. Insert crisper plate in pan and pan in unit. Preheat unit by selecting ROAST, setting temperature to 160°C and setting time to 5 minutes. Select START/STOP to begin.
3. In a bowl, stir together walnuts, jelly, honey, cinnamon, salt and soaked sultanas. Set aside.
4. Place apples onto a large sheet of aluminum foil, folding up edges to create a bowl.
5. Place foil with apples into the unit. Using a small spoon, stuff walnut filling equally into the center of each apple and top each with a piece of butter. Select ROAST, set temperature to 160°C and set time to 25 minutes. Select START/STOP to begin.
6. While apples are cooking, combine confectioners' sugar, milk and vanilla in a small bowl.

7. After 20 minutes, remove pan from unit. Drizzle confectioners' sugar mixture evenly over each apple. Reinsert pan and select START/STOP to resume cooking.
8. When cooking is complete, remove foil and allow apples to cool briefly. Serve warm, spooning sauce over apples.

Air Fryer Caramelized Bananas
Servings: 4
Cooking Time: 10 Minutes

Ingredients:
- 2 large bananas, peeled and cut into 1/2 inch slices
- 1 tablespoon salted butter, melted
- 1/2 teaspoon vanilla extract
- 1 tablespoon brown sugar
- 1/2 teaspoon ground cinnamon

Directions:
1. Preheat air fryer to 390 degrees F (195 degrees C)
2. Spread out banana slices on a plate. Combine butter and vanilla extract and drizzle over the bananas.
3. Combine brown sugar and cinnamon. Sprinkle half of the sugar mixture over the slices, flip, and sprinkle the remaining sugar over the other side. Make sure both sides are well coated.
4. Spray the air fryer basket with cooking spray or line with a parchment paper.
5. Place banana slices in the air fryer basket in a single layer
6. making sure not to overcrowd or overlap. Cook until golden brown and caramelized to your liking, 7 to 9 minutes. You do not need to flip banana slices over.
7. Remove bananas from the basket, cool slightly, and serve.

Notes
Depending on the size of your air fryer you may need to fry bananas in batches.
Cooking time may vary depending on the size and brand of your air fryer. If you are only have unsalted butter, add a pinch of salt.

Easy Air Fryer Donuts
Servings: 10
Cooking Time: 10 Minutes

Ingredients:
- 1 can biscuits
- ¼ cup butter melted
- ½ cup sugar
- 1 tablespoon cinnamon

Directions:
1. Preheat air fryer to 350°F.
2. Cut a circle out of the center of each biscuit using a small 1" cutter.
3. Place 4-5 pieces of the dough in the air fryer.
4. Cook 3 minutes. Flip and cook an additional 2-3 minutes or until browned.
5. Remove from the air fryer and while warm, brush with butter. Combine sugar & cinnamon, toss donuts in sugar mixture.
6. Repeat with remaining donuts. Once the donuts are cooked, add the donut holes to the air fryer and cook for 3 minutes. Toss with additional butter and sugar if desired.
7. Notes
8. If you don't have a 1" cutter, the center can be cut using a large pastry tip.
9. Donuts can be cooled and glazed or dipped in glaze if preferred.

Key Lime Pie
Servings: 6
Cooking Time: 20 Minutes

Ingredients:
- 6 graham crackers
- 3 tablespoons unsalted butter, melted
- 1 tablespoon granulated sugar
- 4 large egg yolks
- 1 can sweetened condensed milk
- ½ cup key lime juice
- 1/3 cup creme fraiche
- 1 tablespoon lime zest
- 1 teaspoon vanilla extract
- Toppings
- ½ cup heavy whipping cream
- 2 tablespoons powdered sugar
- Items Needed:
- Food processor
- 7-inch springform pan

- Metal rack accessory

Directions:
1. Place the graham crackers in the bowl of a food processor fitted with the blade attachment, then blend until the crackers are broken down into crumbs.
2. Pour the crumbs into a bowl and mix with the granulated sugar and melted butter. Press the mixture into the bottom of a 7-inch springform pan, then freeze for 20 minutes.
3. Whisk the egg yolks until they have turned a light shade of yellow, then whisk in the condensed milk until the mixture is thickened. Gradually whisk in the key lime juice, crème fraiche, lime zest, and vanilla extract.
4. Remove the springform pan from the freezer and pour the pie filling over the crust.
5. Pour 1 ½ cups of water into the inner pot of the pressure cooker and place the metal rack accessory into the pot, then place the springform pan onto the rack.
6. Place the lid onto the pressure cooker and slide the vent switch to Seal.
7. Select the Pressure Cook function and press Keep Warm to disable.
8. Adjust pressure to high and time to 15 minutes, then press Start.
9. Release pressure naturally for 5 minutes by leaving the pressure cooker alone, then slide the vent switch to Vent to quickly release the remaining pressure.
10. Open the lid carefully and lift the rack out of the inner pot, then let the pie cool to room temperature before placing it in the refrigerator to chill for at least 6 hours.
11. Beat the whipped cream and powdered sugar to stiff peaks and reserve for a garnish.
12. Serve the key lime pie cold, cut into wedges, garnished with dollops of whipped cream.

Air Fryer Grilled Cheese
Servings: 2
Cooking Time: 5 Minutes

Ingredients:
- 4 slices sandwich bread or sourdough bread
- 4 ounces sharp cheddar
- 2 tablespoons butter

Directions:
1. Preheat the air fryer to 350°F.
2. Butter one side of each slice of bread. Place the cheese between two slices of bread, with the buttered side facing out.
3. Place the sandwiches in the air fryer basket in a single layer.
4. Cook for 4-6 minutes, or until the bread is golden brown and the cheese is melted.

Notes

Tip: If the bread (or cheese) is thin or light, it might blow off the sandwich while cooking. To ensure your sandwich stays together, use thicker bread and cheese, or lightly butter both sides of the bread. You may also secure it with toothpicks.

Cooking time: Air fryers can vary, you may need to cook your sandwiches for a minute more or less.

Variations: Swap out the cheddar for any cheese you have on hand. A pinch of garlic powder can be added to the outside of the bread. Add in your favorites. Bacon, tomato slices, jalapenos, the possibilities are endless.

Zucchini Chocolate Chip Cookies
Servings: 2
Cooking Time: 10 Minutes

Ingredients:
- 1 1/2 c. all-purpose flour
- 1/4 tsp. kosher salt
- 1/4 tsp. baking soda
- 1/4 tsp. ground cinnamon
- 5 tbsp. butter, softened
- 1/2 c. granulated sugar
- 1/2 c. packed brown sugar
- 1 large egg
- 1/4 c. plain Greek yogurt
- 1 tsp. vanilla extract
- 1 c. shredded zuccini
- 1 c. semi-sweet chocolate chips
- 1 c. old-fashioned oats

Directions:
1. FOR OVEN

2. Preheat oven to 350°. In a small bowl, whisk together flour, salt, baking soda and cinnamon.
3. In a large bowl, beat together sugars and butter until light and fluffy. Add egg, yogurt, and vanilla and mix until evenly combined. Mix in flour mixture until just combined. Fold in oats, chocolate chips, and zucchini. Drop by rounded teaspoon 2 inches apart on baking sheets.
4. Bake for 15 minutes. Let cool for 2 minutes on baking sheet and transfer to wire rack to cool completely. Note: Cookies will spread a bit, but not take on much color.
5. FOR AIR FRYER
6. In a small bowl, whisk together flour, salt, baking soda and cinnamon.
7. In a large bowl, beat together sugars and butter until light and fluffy. Add egg, yogurt, and vanilla and mix until evenly combined. Mix in flour mixture until just combined. Fold in oats, chocolate chips, and zucchini.
8. Line air fryer basket with parchment paper. Working in batches, use a small cookie scoop to scoop dough and place on parchment paper at least 1" apart.
9. Cook at 350° for 10 minutes?! Remove cookies and let cool on a wire rack, and repeat with remaining dough. Note: Cookies will not spread much, but will get golden brown.

Cranberry Orange Sweet Rolls
Ingredients:
- (dough ingredients)
- 3 1/2 cups all purpose flour
- 2 1/4 tsp instant dry yeast
- Zest of one orange
- 1/3 cup butter
- 1/3 cup sugar
- 3/4 tsp salt
- 1 1/4 cups milk
- 1 egg
- (filing ingredients)
- 2 cups fresh cranberries, whole and chopped
- 1/2 cup granulated sugar
- zest and juice of one orange
- 1/4 cup butter melted (use 1/3 cup cranberry jelly in place of the butter, if desired)
- 1-2 tsp olive oil for rolling out dough
- Butter for greasing the pan
- (glaze ingredients)
- 3 tablespoons orange juice
- 1 cup powdered sugar

Directions:
1. In a large bowl, mix the all purpose flour and the yeast. Add the orange zest into the flour mixture.
2. Next, melt 1/3 cup butter in a saucepan over medium heat. Once it's melted and starts to bubble, turn off the heat and stir in the sugar and the salt until the grains begin to dissolve in the hot butter. Add the milk slowly, stirring constantly. Once it feels only slightly warm to the touch (slightly above room temperature) you're good to add in the egg and whisk it into the mixture.
3. Pour the wet ingredients into the dry ingredients.
4. Using the dough hooks, mix on low and watch the ingredients combine. After about a minute you should see a sticky dough starting to come together. If you need to turn the mixer off and scrape down the sides and bottom of the bowl, you can.
5. Turn up the mixer speed slightly and allow the mixture to knead the dough for about 3 minutes. The dough should be tacky to the touch, but not so sticky that it's very messy. It should pull away from the sides of the bowl easily. If the dough appears too sticky, continue kneading and add flour, one tablespoon at a time, until the dough reaches that tacky texture.
6. Cover the bowl with some plastic wrap and move it to a warm place in your kitchen to rise for about 1 1/2 to 2 hours.
7. To make the filling: add the chopped and whole cranberries to a large bowl and stir them together with the sugar, orange zest and orange juice.
8. After the dough has risen fully, turn the dough out onto a work surface that's been

very lightly greased with vegetable oil. Using a rolling pin, roll out the dough evenly until you have a rectangle shape. Brush the dough with the melted butter (or cranberry jelly, if using this instead).

9. Spread the cranberry mixture evenly over the rectangle of dough.
10. Roll up the dough from the long side until you've got one long roll. Cut the roll at an even thickness as this promotes even baking.
11. Grease baking pan with some butter. Arrange the pieces in the pan you've greased. An arrangement of about 7-8 rolls.
12. Preheat the Air Fryer Oven to 350°F.
13. Once the oven has preheated, bake for about 25-30 minutes, or until they're a nice even light golden brown color.
14. Remove the pan from the oven and let them cool on the pan for about 20-25 minutes.
15. While the buns are cooling, begin making the glaze by mixing together the powdered sugar and orange juice, just until a drizzle-consistency is reached.
16. Drizzle the glaze over the buns when they're cooled almost completely.
17. Sprinkle some additional cranberries and orange zest over the top, and serve!

Frozen Grands Biscuits In Air Fryer
Servings: 6
Cooking Time: 22 Minutes

Ingredients:
- 6 Frozen Grands Biscuits
- oil spray
- butter and/or jam , optional

Directions:
1. Spray the air fryer basket or racks with oil to keep the biscuits from sticking. We don't suggest using parchment paper underneath because you want maximum air flow under the biscuits to help them cook all the way though. The parchment paper prevents maximum air flow under the biscuits.
2. Lay biscuits in single layer of air fryer basket or racks. Make sure to space them out so they aren't touching & have room to rise & expand. Cook in batches if needed.
3. Spray the tops of the biscuits to give them a more golden top when they air fry.
4. Air Fry at 330°F/165°C for 10 minutes. Gently wiggle the biscuits to loosen from the baskets. Flip the biscuits over.
5. Continue to Air Fry at 330°F/165°C for another 8-12 minutes, or until golden and cooked through. If they're still slightly doughy in the middle, leave them in the turned-off air fryer for about 2-3 minutes to continue cooking in the residual heat. Serve with butter or jam if desired.

Air Fryer Oreo
Servings: 4
Cooking Time: 5 Minutes

Ingredients:
- 8 Oreos or other sandwich cookies
- 1 package Pillsbury Crescents Rolls (or crescent dough sheet)
- Powdered sugar for dusting (optional)

Directions:
1. Spread out crescent dough onto a cutting board or counter.
2. Using your finger, press down into each perforated line so it forms one big sheet. Cut into eighths.
3. Place an Oreo cookie in the center of each of the crescent roll squares and roll each corner up.
4. Bunch up the rest of the crescent roll to make sure it covers the entire Oreo cookie. Do not stretch the crescent roll too thin or it will break.
5. Preheat your air fryer to 320 degrees.
6. Gently place the Air Fried Oreos inside the air fryer in one even row so they do not touch.
7. Cook Oreos for 5-6 minutes until golden brown on the outside.
8. Carefully remove the Air Fryer Oreos from the air fryer and immediately dust them with powdered sugar if desired.

Peppermint Cookies

Ingredients:
- 1/2 cup butter, softened
- 1/4 cup confectioners sugar
- 1/4 tsp peppermint extract
- 1/2 cup + 2 Tbsp flour
- 1/4 cup cornstarch
- 1 cup vanilla frosting, store bought or homemade
- Red food coloring
- Peppermint candies, crushed

Directions:
1. Preheat your air fryer oven to 350°F.
2. In a mixing bowl, add the softened butter, confectioners sugar and peppermint extract and mix. Set aside.
3. In another bowl, whisk together the flour and cornstarch.
4. Next, add in the wet ingredients in with the dry ingredients. This will make a crumbly dough.
5. Refrigerate for about 30 minutes.
6. Grease the air fryer's baking sheet.
7. Remove the dough from the refrigerator and roll into 6 regular sized cookie balls or about 8-10 small cookies.
8. Bake for 10 minutes then cool on a rack for at least 10 minutes.
9. Take your 1 cup of frosting and combine 1-2 drops of red food coloring to make a subtle reddish, pinky color.
10. Put the peppermint candies in a baggy and crush.
11. Frost the tops of each cookie and sprinkle with the crushed peppermint candies!

Air Fryer Blueberry Scones

Servings: 16
Cooking Time: 6 Minutes

Ingredients:
- 1/3 cup butter slightly softened
- 1 3/4 cups all purpose flour
- 1/4 cup sugar
- 2 teaspoon baking powder
- 1 large egg
- 3/4 cup fresh or frozen blueberries
- 4 tablespoon milk

Directions:
1. In a medium bowl, combine the butter, flour, sugar, and baking powder. Stir until it become crumbly.
2. Add in the egg, and the milk, one tablespoon at a time, until the dough forms.
3. Stir in the blueberries.
4. Roll the dough, until it is about ½ inch thick. Cut with 2 inch cutter.
5. Place in air fryer basket on parchment paper, or lightly brushed with olive oil.
6. Cook at 380 degrees Fahrenheit for 5-6 minutes, until they are golden.

NOTES
Do not use air fryer with just parchment paper by itself. It must be weighted down by the, or it can be a fire hazard!

4-ingredient Air Fryer Cookies

Servings: 6
Cooking Time: 10 Minutes

Ingredients:
- 100g/3½oz hazelnut chocolate spread
- 75g/2¾oz plain flour
- 3 tbsp full-fat milk
- 40g/1½oz chocolate (any type), melted, to decorate

Directions:
1. Preheat the air fryer to 180C. Place the chocolate spread, flour and milk in a bowl. Mix well and then, using your hands, bring together to make a firm dough.
2. Roll the mixture into 6 evenly sized balls then flatten into cookies. Lay a sheet of baking paper in the air fryer basket then place the cookies on top, leaving a little space between each one.
3. Air fry for 8–10 minutes then carefully lift out. Drizzle over the melted chocolate and leave to cool before serving.

NOTES
If you don't have an air fryer, you can cook these in an oven preheated to 200C/180C Fan/Gas 6 for 12–14 minutes.
You may find the mixture easier to roll if you chill the hazelnut chocolate spread before using.

You could also chill the dough in the fridge before baking.

Use plain chocolate spread if you like and decorate them anyway you want to.

Air Fryer Apple Pie Bombs

Servings: 6
Cooking Time: 10 Minutes

Ingredients:
- 15 oz Apple Pie Filling
- 12 oz Biscuit dough
- 4 tbsp granulated white sugar
- 1 tsp cinnamon

Directions:
1. Open the biscuit dough and remove the biscuits from the container. Split the biscuits in half and separate dough. Spread them out slightly with your hands or with a rolling pin.
2. Open the apple pie filling and scoop a tablespoon of apple pie filling into the center of each circle. Fold in the sides, and then cover with the other half of the dough, forming a ball.
3. Roll the dough to continue to round out the ball and pinch the seams and then set aside. Continue making the rest of the apple pie bombs.
4. Combine the cinnamon and sugar mixture into a small bowl. Dip each dough ball into the cinnamon sugar mixture.
5. Add parchment paper to the bottom of air fryer basket and add the dough balls on the top, place seam side down in a single layer. Make sure to leave 2 inches in between each one. You may have to cook these in two batches. You can also use cooking spray if you don't have parchment paper.
6. Add the basket to the air fryer and cook on 350 degrees Fahrenheit for 8-10 minutes, turning them about halfway through, and then again for the last minute. Add an additional minute if needed.
7. Remove from the air fryer when they are fully cooked and a nice golden brown.

NOTES
I like to use grand biscuits, but If you don't have a can of store-bought biscuit dough you can use canned crescent rolls or make your own homemade biscuit dough.

Store leftover apple pie bombs in an airtight container in the refrigerator for up to 3 days. To reheat, place into the air fryer and cook at 350 degrees Fahrenheit for 3 minutes, or until heated through.

You can eat these small desserts all by themselves, or serve them fresh with vanilla ice cream and top with brown sugar.

Homemade Strawberry Twists

Ingredients:
- 5 oz date paste
- 1.2 oz freeze-dried strawberries
- 3 scoops collagen peptides (optional)

Directions:
1. Soak dates for at least 30 minutes, up to eight hours. Drain and use a blender or food processor to blend until smooth.
2. Combine date paste, strawberries, and collagen powder (if using) into the food processor or blender.
3. Process the ingredients together until you have a thick fruit paste.
4. Prep your Air Fryer Oven trays with aluminum foil. We recommend poking small holes on edges to ensure that air can circulate.
5. Once you have your batter made, you can pipe it out onto trays.
6. Dehydrate the twists at 125 degrees F for 18-24 hours.
7. Store in an airtight container. Enjoy!

Air Fryer Vanilla Glazed Donuts

Servings: 8
Cooking Time: 6 Minutes

Ingredients:
- 1 can biscuits
- Vanilla Glaze
- ¼ cup powdered sugar
- ¼ teaspoon vanilla extract
- 1 tablespoon milk
- 1 tablespoon sprinkles optional

Directions:

1. Preheat air fryer to 350°F.
2. Mix all glaze ingredients together and set them aside.
3. Using a small circular cutter remove the center of the biscuit.
4. Place in the air fryer basket and cook for 3 minutes, flip the donuts and cook for another 2-3 minutes or until golden brown.
5. Allow donuts to cool completely then dip into the glaze and top with sprinkles if desired.

Strawberry Pretzel Pie
Servings: 8

Ingredients:
- Pie Crust
- 1 cup fine pretzel crumbs
- 6 tablespoons butter, melted
- 2 tablespoons brown sugar
- 2 tablespoons maple syrup
- Items Needed
- 8-inch springform pan
- Stand mixer fitted with the paddle attachment
- Filling
- 16 ounces cream cheese, softened to room temperature
- ⅔ cup powdered sugar
- 1½ teaspoon vanilla extract
- ¼ teaspoon rose water
- 1½ cups heavy whipping cream
- ½ cup strawberry preserves
- 2 cups fresh strawberries, sliced, for garnish
- Fresh mint, torn, for garnish

Directions:
1. Place the pretzel crumbs, butter, brown sugar, and maple syrup in a medium bowl and mix until combined and the texture is like that of wet sand.
2. Pack the mixture into the bottom of an 8-inch springform pan.
3. Place the crisper plate into the Smart Air Fryer basket, then place the springform pan onto the crisper plate.
4. Select the Bake function, adjust time to 8 minutes, then press Start/Pause.

5. Remove the pie crust when done and let cool completely.
6. Place the cream cheese, powdered sugar, vanilla extract, and rose water into the bowl of a stand mixer fitted with the paddle attachment and mix on high until combined, then add the heavy whipping cream and continue beating until light and fluffy.
7. Remove the bowl from the mixer and stir in the strawberry preserves with a spatula to create a swirl throughout the batter.
8. Pour the filling into the cooled pie crust, then chill in the refrigerator for up to 2 days or until set.
9. Top the pie with fresh strawberries and mint before serving, then carefully remove from the springform pan, slice, and serve.

Lemon Meringue Cupcakes
Servings: 4
Cooking Time: 12 Minutes

Ingredients:
- 1 1/4 cup flour
- 1 tsp baking powder
- A pinch of salt
- 1/2 cup unsalted butter, room temperature
- 3/4 cup sugar
- 2 eggs
- 2 tsp lemon zest
- 1/2 cup milk
- 4 tbsp store bought lemon curd
- Meringue topping:
- 2 egg whites, room temperature
- 4 tbsp fine white sugar

Directions:
1. Set the air fryer to bake and preheat the air fryer to 180 degrees c.
2. In one bowl, cream the butter and sugar together.
3. Add the eggs and mix until combined.
4. Add the flour, baking powder, lemon zest and salt to the egg mixture and mix well.
5. Place the silicone muffin moulds in the air fryer and fill them with the mixture.

6. Set the timer to 12 minutes and air fry until golden and until a toothpick comes out clean.
7. Remove and allow to cool.
8. To make the meringue icing beat the egg whites until frothy and slowly add the sugar then beat further until the mixture forms stiff peaks.
9. Remove the middle of the cupcake with a small spoon and set aside.
10. Fill the cupcake with lemon curd.
11. Pipe the meringue mixture on the cupcake and put the cupcakes back in the air fryer for 38 seconds to get the golden top.

Blueberry "pop Tarts"

Servings: 4

Ingredients:
- 1 pack (320g) Just Roll Short Crust Pastry
- 120g blueberry preserves (strawberry or black current can be substituted)
- 1 tbsp corn flour
- For dusting Plain flour
- For the topping
- 75g icing sugar
- 1 tbsp water
- To top 100's & 1000's, sprinkles or other topping of choice

Directions:
1. Unroll the pastry sheet, lightly sprinkle with flour and cut into 8 even rectangles (9cm X 11cm)
2. Mix preserves and corn flour and drop about 2 tablespoons in the center of 4 of the rectangles and spread, leaving a border around the edge. Place the remaining rectangles over the filling and press down with fingers lightly. Dock the edges all the way around the tart with a fork. You may need to dip the fork into flour if it sticks. Be sure to seal well.
3. Insert Crisper plate in basket and place basket in unit. Preheat unit by selecting BAKE 160°C to 3 minutes. Select START/STOP to begin
4. Once unit has preheated place 2 tarts at a time in unit and close. Select BAKE, set

temperature to 160°C, and set time for 20 minutes. Select START/STOP to begin. Check after 10 minutes, flip over with tongs and cook 10 more minutes until golden on both sides. Remove and cool
5. Mix icing sugar and water and once tarts are completely cooled drizzle with glaze and sprinkles.

Peanut Butter Banana Oat Protein Cookies

Servings: 4
Cooking Time: 20 Minutes

Ingredients:
- 2 medium very ripe bananas
- 1 cup old fashioned oats (or quick oats (check labels for gluten-free))
- 1 scoop vanilla protein powder (I like Orgain)
- 1 large egg (lightly beaten)
- ¼ teaspoon cinnamon
- Pinch kosher salt
- ½ teaspoon vanilla extract
- ¼ cup peanut butter (or nut butter, or seed butter)
- ¼ cup sugar free chocolate chips (such as Lily's)

Directions:
1. Preheat oven to 350 degrees F. Line 2 sheet pans with parchment or silicon baking mats.
2. Move oven racks to the second from top and second from bottom slots.
3. In a medium bowl, mash the bananas.
4. Add the oats, protein powder, egg, cinnamon, salt, vanilla, and peanut butter and chocolate chips and mix with a fork until combined.
5. Scoop ¼ cup of mixture and place on a baking sheet, flatten the top slightly with the back of the measuring cup. Repeat with remaining mixture, adding 4 cookies to each sheet.
6. Bake for 16 to 20 minutes, rotating pans ½ through bake time to allow for even browning.
7. Allow to cool 5 minutes on the pan then transfer to a wire rack to cool completely.
8. Notes

9. Store in an airtight container in the refrigerator for up to 4 days. Can be eaten warm, cold, at room temperature or warmed in the microwave for 10 seconds.

Air Fryer Homemade Cannoli
Servings: 20

Ingredients:
- FOR THE FILLING:
- 1 (16-oz.) container ricotta
- 1/2 c. mascarpone cheese
- 1/2 c. powdered sugar, divided
- 3/4 c. heavy cream
- 1 tsp. pure vanilla extract
- 1 tsp. orange zest
- 1/4 tsp. kosher salt
- 1/2 c. mini chocolate chips, for garnish
- FOR THE SHELLS:
- 2 c. all-purpose flour, plus more for surface
- 1/4 c. granulated sugar
- 1 tsp. kosher salt
- 1/2 tsp. cinnamon
- 4 tbsp. cold butter, cut into cubes
- 6 tbsp. white wine
- 1 large egg
- 1 egg white, for brushing
- Vegetable oil, for frying
- See All Nutritional Information

Directions:
1. MAKE FILLING:
2. Drain ricotta by placing it a fine mesh strainer set over a large bowl. Let drain in refrigerator for at least an hour and up to overnight.
3. In a large bowl using a hand mixer, beat heavy cream and 1/4 cup powdered sugar until stiff peaks form.
4. In another large bowl, combine ricotta, mascarpone, remaining 1/4 cup powdered sugar, vanilla, orange zest, and salt. Fold in whipped cream. Refrigerate until ready to fill cannoli, at least 1 hour.
5. MAKE SHELLS:
6. In a large bowl, whisk together flour, sugar, salt, and cinnamon. Cut butter into flour mixture with your hands or pastry cutter until pea-sized. Add wine and egg and mix until a dough forms. Knead a few times in bowl to help dough come together. Pat into a flat circle, then wrap in plastic wrap and refrigerate at least 1 hour and up to overnight.
7. On a lightly floured surface, divide dough in half. Roll one half out to ⅛" thick. Use a 4" circle cookie cutter to cut out dough. Repeat with remaining dough. Re-roll scraps to cut a few extra circles.
8. Wrap dough around cannoli molds and brush egg whites where the dough will meet to seal together.
9. FOR FRYING:
10. In a large pot over medium heat, heat about 2" of oil to 360°. Working in batches, add cannoli molds to oil and fry, turning occasionally, until golden, about 4 minutes. Remove from oil and place on a paper towel-lined plate. Let cool slightly.
11. When cool enough to handle or using a kitchen towel to hold, gently twist shells off of molds to remove.
12. Place filling in a pastry bag fitted with an open star tip. Pipe filling into shells, then dip ends in mini chocolate chips.
13. FOR AIR FRYER:
14. Working in batches, place molds in basket of air fryer and cook at 350° for 12 minutes, or until golden.
15. When cool enough to handle or using a kitchen towel to hold, gently remove twist shells off of molds.
16. Place filling in a pastry bag fitted with an open star tip. Pipe filling into shells, then dip ends in mini chocolate chips.

POULTRY RECIPES

Turkey Stuffed Air-fried Peppers

Servings: 3

Ingredients:
- 3 medium red sweet peppers
- 1 tablespoon olive oil
- 12 ounce ground turkey
- ½ cup cooked brown rice
- ¼ cup panko breadcrumbs
- ¾ cup low-sodium marinara sauce
- 3 tablespoon finely chopped flat-leaf parsley
- ¼ teaspoon ground pepper
- ¼ cup grated Parmesan cheese (1 oz.)
- ¼ cup shredded part-skim mozzarella cheese (1 oz.)

Directions:
1. Coat the basket of an air fryer with cooking spray. Cut tops off peppers and reserve. Seed the peppers and set aside.
2. Heat oil in a large skillet over medium-high heat. Add turkey; cook, stirring occasionally, until browned, about 4 minutes. Stir in rice and panko; cook, stirring occasionally, until warmed through, about 1 minute. Remove from heat and stir in marinara, parsley, pepper and Parmesan. Divide the mixture evenly among the prepared peppers.
3. Place the peppers in the prepared air-fryer basket. Nestle the pepper tops in the bottom of the basket. Cook at 350°F until the peppers are tender, about 8 minutes. Top with mozzarella; cook until the cheese is melted, about 2 minutes more.

Air Fryer Chicken Egg Rolls

Servings: 12-14
Cooking Time: 15 Minutes

Ingredients:
- CHICKEN VEGETABLE EGG ROLLS
- 1 pound (454 g) ground chicken (or pork, beef) *see head note
- 2 Tablespoons (30 ml) vegetable oil
- 3 cloves garlic , minced or crushed
- 1 teaspoon (5 ml) freshly grated ginger root , optional
- 1 Tablespoon (15 ml) soy sauce (or fish sauce for more flavor)
- 1/2 teaspoon (2.5 ml) sesame seed oil
- 1/2 teaspoon (2.5 ml) kosher salt , or to taste
- freshly grated black pepper
- 2 cups (70 g) cabbage , shredded thin
- 1/2 cup (65 g) grated carrot , (about 1 medium carrot)
- 3 green onions , small chopped
- 1 large egg
- 14 (about) (1 package) egg roll wrappers or sometimes called "spring roll pastry" wrappers in the freezer section of market.
- oil or oil spray , for coating rolls
- HOISIN-PEANUT DIP
- 1/2 cup (140 g) hoisin
- 1/4 cup (65 g) peanut butter
- chili hot sauce or Sriracha Sauce (optional)
- 1/2 teaspoon (2.5 ml) sesame oil , or to taste
- 2 teaspoons (5 ml) vinegar , or to taste
- about 1/2 cup water , or to preferred dip consistency
- EQUIPMENT
- Air Fryer

Directions:
1. MAKE THE EGG ROLL FILLING
2. Cook the filling: Heat a pan over medium-high heat. Add the oil and then add the garlic and optional ginger. Cook for about 1 minute or until lightly browned. Add the ground chicken, soy sauce, sesame seed oil, salt and pepper. Cook for 1-2 minutes or until the chicken is lightly browned.
3. Add the veggies: cabbage, carrots, and green onions. Cook for another 1-2 minutes or until the vegetables soften. Stir in the egg and cook for another 30 seconds. Remove from heat, place the cooked filling in a colander to drain excess juices and allow to cool.
4. MAKE THE HOISIN-PEANUT DIP
5. Make the dip while the chicken filling is cooling. In bowl, combine all ingredients (hoisin, peanut butter, hot sauce, sesame oil, water, and vinegar) and whisk together. If you are making a very large batch, you

can use a blender by blending all the ingredients together. But make sure you add enough water because some brands of hoisin are very thick.

6. HOW TO ROLL AND AIR FRY
7. Using egg roll wrappers or spring roll wrappers, add about 1-2 Tablespoons of chicken filling to each wrapper (depending on the size of the wrapper) Tuck and roll the wrapper around the filling.
8. Brush the top corner of the wrapper with water or beaten egg to help seal the wrapper end, and then finish rolling the egg roll. Repeat for all the egg rolls. Brush or spray rolls with oil to coat
9. Air Fry at 380°F/195°C for 8 minutes. Flip the egg rolls. If they look dry, spray the egg rolls with oil again.
10. Continue air frying for 6 minutes or until the wrapper is crispy and browned. If needed add another 1-2 minutes. If you use the larger wrapper cook a little longer so that all the layers can cook through to avoid being tough and chewy.
11. Serve warm with hoisin-peanut dip. You can also wrap these chicken vegetable egg rolls in lettuce and eat them as lettuce egg roll wraps!

Air-fryer Southern-style Chicken
Servings: 6
Cooking Time: 20 Minutes

Ingredients:
- 2 cups crushed Ritz crackers (about 50)
- 1 tablespoon minced fresh parsley
- 1 teaspoon garlic salt
- 1 teaspoon paprika
- 1/2 teaspoon pepper
- 1/4 teaspoon ground cumin
- 1/4 teaspoon rubbed sage
- 1 large egg, beaten
- 1 broiler/fryer chicken (3 to 4 pounds), cut up
- Cooking spray

Directions:
1. Preheat air fryer to 375°. In a shallow bowl, mix the first 7 ingredients. Place egg in a

separate shallow bowl. Dip chicken in egg, then in cracker mixture, patting to help coating adhere. In batches, place chicken in a single layer on greased tray in air-fryer basket; spritz with cooking spray.
2. Cook 10 minutes. Turn chicken and spritz with cooking spray. Cook until chicken is golden brown and juices run clear, 10-20 minutes longer.

Air Fryer Nashville Hot Chicken Hack
Servings: 2
Cooking Time: 20 Minutes

Ingredients:
- FOR THE CHICKEN:
- About 2-4 frozen pre-cooked breaded chicken breasts
- FOR THE NASHVILLE HOT SAUCE:
- 1/4 cup (60 g) butter
- 1/4 cup (60 ml) oil
- 1 Tablespoon (15 ml) ground cayenne pepper , or 2 Tablespoons for extra hot
- 2 Tablespoons (30 ml) brown sugar
- 1 teaspoon (5 ml) garlic powder
- 1 teaspoon (5 ml) paprika
- 1 Tablespoon (15 ml) Worcestershire sauce or soy sauce
- 1/2 teaspoon (2.5 ml) salt , or to taste
- 1 teaspoon (5 ml) black pepper
- FOR SERVING
- 6-8 slices (6-8 slices) white bread
- Pickles , whatever you prefer - bread & butter, dill, or both
- EQUIPMENT
- Air Fryer

Directions:
1. Make the Sauce: Combine all the sauce ingredients in a bowl or saucepan (butter, oil, cayenne pepper, brown sugar, garlic powder, paprika, Worcestershire or soy sauce, salt and pepper). Microwave or heat until butter is just melted (the hotter it is, the harder it will be to emulsify the spices in the liquids). Whisk thoroughly until smooth.
2. When the sauce is cooler, it doesn't separate as easily so we like to brush sauce on the

chicken when the sauce is slightly cooler or room temperature. If you want your sauce warmer, then keep stirring or whisking the sauce as you brush the chicken so that you have as little separation of sauce/oil as possible. The warmer the sauce is, the more the spices will want to separate from the liquids.

3. Place the frozen breaded chicken breasts in the air fryer basket in a single layer. Make sure they aren't overlapping. No oil spray is needed.

4. Air Fry at 380°F/193°C for 10 minutes. Flip the chicken over.

5. Continue to Air Fry at 380°F/193°C for another 2 minutes. Check the chicken breasts and if needed, add another 2-3 minutes or until heated through and crispy to your preference.

6. Place chicken on top of white bread. Brush both sides of chicken with the hot sauce. Top with pickles and serve warm. Enjoy!

NOTES

Air Frying Tips and Notes:

No Oil Necessary. Cook Frozen - Do not thaw first.

Don't overcrowd the air fryer basket. Lay in a single layer.

Recipe timing is based on a non-preheated air fryer. If cooking in multiple batches of chicken back to back, the following batches may cook a little quicker.

Recipes were tested in 3.7 to 6 qt. air fryers. If using a larger air fryer, the chicken might cook quicker so adjust cooking time.

Remember to set a timer to flip/toss as directed in recipe.

Chicken Parmesan With Quick Garlic Pull-apart Rolls

Servings: 4
Cooking Time: 20 Minutes

Ingredients:
- Quick Garlic Pull-apart Rolls
- 3 cups self-raising flour
- 1 cup full cream plain yoghurt
- 1/2 cup melted butter

- 4 cloves garlic, crushed
- 1/2 Tbsp chopped parsley
- Pinch of salt
- 2 chicken breasts, halved lengthways
- 1/3 cup flour
- 1/2 tsp each onion powder and paprika
- 2 large eggs, whisked
- 1 cup breadcrumbs
- 1/4 cup freshly grated Parmesan cheese
- 1 tsp dried oregano
- salt and pepper to taste
- Cheats Marinara sauce
- 1 cup tinned chopped tomatoes
- 1 Tbsp olive oil
- 1 garlic clove, crushed
- 1/2 tsp each salt and dried basil
- 1/4 tsp ground pepper
- 1 cup grated mozzarella
- fresh basil, for garnish

Directions:
1. Start with the quick rolls: combine the flour, salt and yoghurt in a medium bowl and knead for 7-8 minutes until a smooth dough is formed. Cut into 8 balls and place in a greased dish that fits the Vortex Dual drawer. Cover with a cloth while the drawer heats to the correct temperature.

2. Prepare the coating sequence: place flour, onion powder and paprika in a shallow bowl. Place eggs in a second bowl and in a third combine breadcrumbs, Parmesan and dried oregano.

3. Turn on the Vortex Dual and set drawer 1 to Air Fry 180C for 12 minutes and drawer 2 to Bake at 180C for 20 minutes. Press Sync Finish and Start to commence preheating.

4. Season the chicken breast fillets on both sides. Coat one fillet at a time in the flour mix, then eggs and lastly toss in the breadcrumbs and press gently to ensure the crumbs are well adhered.

5. Add all 4 crumbed fillets to drawer 1 and cook for 7 minutes, turn half way through the cook time.

6. Add the rolls to drawer 2 to Bake.

7. For the cheats marinara, combine the ingredients in a medium bowl and use a

fork to mash the tomato chunks and mix all the ingredients.

8. With 5 minutes left, open the drawer and top the crumbed chicken fillets with the sauce and grated mozzarella allow to cook until the cheese is melted.

9. Combine the melted butter, garlic and parsley in a small bowl and when the rolls are 5 minutes from the end brush over the top.

10. When all the cooking has ended, remove the chicken fillets and garlic rolls, brush over more garlic and herb butter and serve with a leafy side salad and garnished with basil.

Air Fryer Chili Crisp Crunch Chicken Wings

Servings: 4
Cooking Time: 30 Minutes

Ingredients:
- 2 pounds (907 g) chicken wings
- Kosher salt , or sea salt, to taste
- black pepper , to taste
- garlic powder , optional
- 1/4 cup chili crisp crunch , or to taste
- OPTIONAL - FOR EXTRA CRISPY CORN STARCH CRUST
- 1/4 cup (30 g) corn starch , or as needed
- oil spray , as needed
- EQUIPMENT
- Air Fryer
- Oil Sprayer optional

Directions:
1. If you have whole wings, separate them into the drum and flat. If needed, pat dry the chicken wings. Season with salt, pepper, and optional garlic powder.

2. For oil-free version, place in even layer in air fryer basket/tray. Follow air fry instructions below. For Extra Crispy Crust, follow optional steps for corn starch crust.

3. FOR EXTRA CRISPY CORN STARCH CRUST

4. Add seasoning to the wings then lay them in single layer on a plate or cutting board. Sprinkle cornstarch over the wings on both sides.

5. Liberally spray wings evenly with oil spray so that all the cornstarch is coated in oil. There should be no dry white clumps of cornstarch or else they will cook hard and dry.

6. Place the coated wings in your air fryer basket or tray/rack.

7. AIR FRY

8. Air Fry wings at 400°F/205°C for 20 minutes minutes or until crispy-looking and nearly cooked through.

9. Flip the wings and Air Fry at 400°F/205°C for additional 5-10 minutes or until wings are fully cooked and crispy.

10. Toss with the chili crisp/crunch to taste. Spiciness will vary greatly on the brand of chili crisp/crunch, as well has how much you use on the wings. Adjust to your preference.

NOTES

No Oil Necessary. The wings have enough fat in the skin to crisp up nicely on their own.

Shake several times for even cooking.

Don't overcrowd fryer basket.

If using a sauce, it is added in just at the end, otherwise it often burns before the chicken wings are cooked.

Recipes were cooked in 3-4 qt air fryers. If using a larger air fryer, the recipe might cook quicker so adjust cooking time.

If cooking in multiple batches, the first batch will take longer to cook if Air Fryer is not already pre-heated.

Remember to set a timer to shake/flip/toss the food as directed in recipe.

Air Fryer Doritos Crusted Chicken Strips

Servings: 6
Cooking Time: 25 Minutes

Ingredients:
- 9 oz. (255 g) Doritos or any flavor tortilla chips
- 1 large egg , beaten (or more if needed)
- 2 pounds (907 g) chicken , cut into thin strips
- 1 teaspoon (5 ml) garlic powder

- 1/2 teaspoon (2.5 ml) salt
- fresh black pepper , to taste
- For dipping: Ranch, sour cream, ketchup, bbq sauce or your favorite sauce
- EQUIPMENT
- Air Fryer

Directions:
1. Crush the Doritos or tortilla chips in a bag with a rolling pin. Crush them thoroughly. The smaller the pieces, the better they'll coat the chicken. Place the crushed chips in a bowl for dredging the chicken. Put the beaten egg in another bowl.
2. Season the chicken strips with garlic powder, salt and pepper.
3. Working with one or two chicken strips at a time, first coat the chicken strips with the egg, then coat with the crushed Doritos. Gently press the chicken into the crushed chips, then pour chip pieces over the chicken strips. Gently press chips into chicken. This help chips to stay dry. If they're wet, they stick less to the chicken.
4. Pre-heat your Air Fryer at 380°F (195°C) for 4 minutes. Spray the air fryer basket or racks with oil spray. Gently lay chicken pieces in the basket or on the racks in a single layer (cook in batches if needed). Spray oil spray on top of coated chicken.
5. Air Fry at 380°F (195°C) for 15 minutes. Gently turn the chicken pieces and spray the tops with oil spray (make sure to turn the chicken gently or else the chip pieces will fall off).
6. Air Fry for additional 3-5 minutes or until the crust is crispy golden brown and chicken is cooked through. Serve warm with your favorite dip.

Air Fryer Bbq Chicken Wings

Servings: 2-4
Cooking Time: 25 Minutes

Ingredients:
- 1 ½ lbs of chicken wings, wings and flats separated, tips discarded
- 2 teaspoons Stubbs BBQ rub
- ¼ - ½ cup BBQ sauce

Directions:
1. Preheat your air fryer to 380 degrees F.
2. Pat the chicken wings dry and coat them evenly with the BBQ rub.
3. Place the wings in the air fryer basket in a single layer, leaving room between the wings.
4. Cook for 20 minutes, flipping the wings halfway through.
5. Turn the temperature to 400 degrees and cook for another 3 to 5 minutes.
6. Remove the wings from the air fryer and toss them in the BBQ sauce. Return to your air fryer for another 1 to 2 minutes to heat up the sauce, or serve right away.
7. Remove the BBQ chicken wings from the air fryer and enjoy!

NOTES
HOW TO REHEAT CHICKEN WINGS IN THE AIR FRYER:
Preheat your air fryer to 350 degrees.
Place leftover wings in the air fryer not touching and cook for 2 to 3 minutes until warmed thoroughly. If already sauced, use an air fryer pan, parchment paper, or silicone basket to help with clean up.
HOW TO COOK FROZEN BBQ WINGS IN THE AIR FRYER:
Preheat your air fryer to 400 degrees.
Toss the wings in BBQ rub then place them in the air fryer and cook for about 30 to 35 minutes, flipping halfway through.
Toss in BBQ sauce, then return to the air fryer for another 2 minutes then enjoy!

Air-fryer Crispy Salt And Pepper Chicken Wings Recipe

Servings: 4
Cooking Time: 20 Minutes

Ingredients:
- 1kg-1.2kg pack Willow Farm chicken wings (about 16 wings)1kg-1.2kg pack Willow Farm Chicken wings (about 16 wings)
- 1 tsp sesame oil
- 1 tsp Shaoxing rice wine or Japanese mirin
- 30g plain flour
- ½ tsp white pepper

- ¼ tsp ground ginger
- sunflower oil spray
- 1 red chilli, thinly sliced
- 2-3 cloves of garlic, chopped
- 2 spring onions, thinly sliced
- For the dipping sauce
- 4 tbsp light mayo
- 100g natural yogurt
- 1 tbsp rice vinegar
- 1 tsp light soy sauce
- 1 tbsp caster sugar
- 2 tsp mild curry powder

Directions:
1. Preheat the air-fryer to 180°C.
2. In a large bowl, toss the chicken wings with the sesame oil and rice wine or mirin. Sprinkle over the flour, the white pepper, ground ginger, and some salt and black pepper, tossing until evenly coated.
3. Working in 2 batches, spray the basket of the air-fryer with a little oil and arrange half the chicken wings in a single layer with some space between them. Spray with oil and cook for 10 mins.
4. Tip into clean bowl and cook the next batch.
5. Put the sliced chilli, garlic and spring onion into the bowl with both batches of part-cooked chicken wings and shake to coat. Add everything from the bowl back into the air-fryer and cook for 10-15 mins, until dark golden brown and cooked through.
6. Meanwhile, stir together the ingredients for the dipping sauce, cover and chill for 10 mins before serving with the cooked chicken wings.

Air-fryer Chicken Tenders

Servings: 4
Cooking Time: 15 Minutes

Ingredients:
- 1/2 cup panko bread crumbs
- 1/2 cup potato sticks, crushed
- 1/2 cup crushed cheese crackers
- 1/4 cup grated Parmesan cheese
- 2 bacon strips, cooked and crumbled
- 2 teaspoons minced fresh chives
- 1/4 cup butter, melted

- 1 tablespoon sour cream
- 1 pound chicken tenderloins
- Additional sour cream and chives

Directions:
1. Preheat air fryer to 400°. In a shallow bowl, combine the first 6 ingredients. In another shallow bowl, whisk butter and sour cream. Dip chicken in butter mixture, then in crumb mixture, patting to help coating adhere.
2. In batches, arrange chicken in a single layer on greased tray in air-fryer basket; spritz with cooking spray. Cook until coating is golden brown and chicken is no longer pink, 7-8 minutes on each side. Serve with additional sour cream and chives.

Air Fryer Chicken Parmesan Recipe

Servings: 4
Cooking Time: 12 Minutes

Ingredients:
- 1/4 cup all-purpose flour
- 1/2 teaspoon garlic powder
- 1/2 teaspoon onion powder
- 1/2 cup panko breadcrumbs
- 2 ounces Parmesan cheese, grated (1 cup loosely packed or 1/2 cup store-bought)
- 2 large eggs
- 2 boneless, skinless chicken breasts (about 1 1/2 pounds total)
- 3/4 teaspoon kosher salt
- 1/4 teaspoon freshly ground black pepper
- Cooking spray
- 4 slices part-skim, low-moisture mozzarella cheese (about 4 ounces total)
- 1 cup store-bought or homemade marinara sauce
- Fresh basil leaves, for serving (optional)

Directions:
1. Place 1/4 cup all-purpose flour, 1/2 teaspoon garlic powder, and 1/2 teaspoon onion powder in a shallow bowl or plate and whisk to combine. Place 1/2 cup panko breadcrumbs and 2 ounces Parmesan cheese to a second shallow bowl or plate and whisk to combine. Add 2 large eggs to

a third shallow bowl or plate and whisk to combine.

2. Slice 2 boneless, skinless chicken breasts in half horizontally (also known as butterflying). Season all over with 3/4 teaspoon kosher salt and 1/4 teaspoon black pepper.

3. Working with one piece of chicken at a time, coat the chicken in the flour mixture, then dip in the egg, letting any excess drip off. Coat in the panko-Parmesan crumbs. Place on a baking sheet or plate in a single layer.

4. Heat an air fryer to 400°F. Place 2 breaded chicken pieces in a single layer in the air fryer basket, making sure they do not overlap. Coat with cooking spray. Air fry until golden and crisp, 5 to 6 minutes.

5. Top each piece of chicken with a slice of mozzarella cheese, and secure each piece of cheese with 2 toothpicks. Air fry until the chicken is golden brown, an instant-read thermometer inserted into the center registers at least 165°F, and the cheese melts, 1 to 2 minutes more.

6. Transfer to a plate and cover loosely with aluminum foil. Repeat air frying the remaining chicken and cheese. When the second batch is almost ready, warm 1 cup marinara sauce on the stovetop over medium heat or in the microwave until warm.

7. To serve, remove the toothpicks, divide the marinara sauce evenly among serving plates, and nestle each serving of chicken Parmesan on top. Garnish with fresh basil leaves, if desired.

8. RECIPE NOTES

9. Storage: Refrigerate leftovers in an airtight container for up to 3 days.

Air Fryer Crumbed Chicken Schnitzel

Servings: 4
Cooking Time: 35 Minutes

Ingredients:
- 8 Coles RSPCA Approved Australian Chicken Thigh Fillets
- 1 cup (80g) panko breadcrumbs
- 45g pkt lemon and herb dukkah
- 2 Coles Australian Free Range Eggs, lightly whisked
- 1/3 cup (50g) plain flour
- 350g pkt Coles Kaleslaw Kit
- Select all ingredients

Directions:
1. Place half the chicken between 2 sheets of plastic wrap. Use a meat mallet or rolling pin to gently pound until 2cm thick. Repeat with the remaining chicken.

2. Combine the breadcrumbs and dukkah in a shallow bowl. Place the egg in a medium bowl. Place the flour on a plate and season. Coat each piece of chicken in flour, shaking off excess. Dip in egg, then in breadcrumb mixture and turn to coat. Transfer to a plate. Cover with plastic wrap and place in the fridge for 30 mins to rest.

3. Preheat air fryer to 200°C. Spray the chicken with olive oil spray. Arrange half the chicken in a single layer in the basket of the air fryer. Cook, turning halfway through cooking, for 16 mins or until golden and cooked through. Transfer to a plate and cover with foil to keep warm. Repeat with remaining chicken.

4. Meanwhile, prepare the kaleslaw kit in a bowl following packet directions.

5. Divide the chicken and kaleslaw among serving plates. Season.

RECIPE NOTES
Allow for 30 minutes chilling time.
SERVE WITH lemon wedges.
On the stove: To make this without an air fryer, cook the chicken in 1cm of olive oil in a large frying pan over medium-high heat for 4-5 mins each side or until cooked through.

Bbq Chicken In Air Fryer

Servings: 4
Cooking Time: 20 Minutes

Ingredients:
- 4-6 pieces chicken drumsticks
- 2 tablespoons brown sugar
- 1 teaspoon garlic powder
- 1 tablespoon olive oil or non-stick spray
- 1/2 cup BBQ Sauce

Directions:

1. To prepare the basket or air fryer trays, brush about ½ tablespoon olive oil or spray with cooking spray.
2. Place the chicken, in a single layer, in the air fryer basket. Avoid stacking or overlapping any pieces of chicken.
3. To prepare the chicken dry rub, use a small bowl and blend together the brown sugar and teaspoon garlic powder. Sprinkle the spice mix over each piece of chicken on both sides. Pat it down until the chicken is well covered.
4. Air fry the chicken at 400 degrees Fahrenheit for 20 minutes cooking time. Flip the chicken over halfway through cooking. Use a meat thermometer to confirm internal temperature of 165 degrees F.
5. Once done cooking, remove chicken pieces from air fryer basket or air fryer trays, and then brush chicken with barbecue sauce on both sides of each piece.
6. Serve immediately.

NOTES

I use a Cosori air fryer to make these BBQ Chicken Drumsticks. 20 minutes was perfect timing 4-6 pieces of chicken. Cook times may vary depending on size, wattage, and thickness of your chicken. You may need to give chicken extra 1-2 minutes of cooking time.

The safest way to confirm doneness when cooking meat is to use a digital meat thermometer like this one. The thickest part of the chicken should have internal temperature of 165 degrees Fahrenheit.

For extra flavor, you can add cayenne pepper or chili powder.

Frozen Chicken Thighs In The Air Fryer

Servings: 4-6
Cooking Time: 30 Minutes

Ingredients:

- 1 1/2 to 2 pounds frozen chicken thighs
- 1 tablespoon McCormick Lemon Pepper Seasoning

Directions:

1. Preheat your air fryer to 380 degrees F.
2. Place separated frozen chicken thighs in the air fryer and cook for 15 minutes until the chicken is just thawed.
3. Remove the chicken from the basket.
4. Spray each thigh with cooking oil, then sprinkle on the lemon pepper seasoning evenly.
5. Return the chicken to the basket and cook for 12-15 additional minutes, flipping once halfway through.
6. Remove the chicken thighs from the air fryer and enjoy with your favorite sides.

NOTES
HOW TO REHEAT CHICKEN THIGHS IN THE AIR FRYER
Preheat the air fryer to 350 degrees F.
Place the leftover chicken thighs in the air fryer.
Cook for 3 to 5 minutes until heated through.
How to Cook Thawed Chicken Thighs in the Air Fryer:
Preheat your air fryer to 380 degrees.
Coat the chicken thighs evenly with Lemon Pepper seasoning then place in the air fryer in a single layer.
Cook for 12 to 15 minutes until chicken reaches 165 degrees.

Air Fryer Chicken, Broccoli, And Onions

Servings: 4
Cooking Time: 20 Minutes

Ingredients:

- 1 pound (454 g) boneless skinless chicken breast or thighs , cut into 1-inch bites sized pieces
- 1/4-1/2 pound (113-227 g) broccoli , cut into florets (1-2 cups)
- 1/2 onion , sliced thick
- 3 Tablespoons (45 ml) vegetable oil or grape seed oil
- 1/2 teaspoon (2.5 ml) garlic powder
- 1 Tablespoon (15 ml) fresh minced ginger
- 1 Tablespoon (15 ml) soy sauce , or to taste (use Tamari for Gluten Free)
- 1 Tablespoon (15 ml) rice vinegar (use distilled white vinegar for Gluten Free)
- 1 teaspoon (5 ml) sesame oil

- 2 teaspoons (10 ml) hot sauce (optional)
- 1/2 teaspoon (2.5 ml) sea salt , or to taste
- black pepper , to taste
- serve with lemon wedges , optional

Directions:

1. AIR FRYING OPTION #1: REGULAR COOKED BROCCOLI
2. Make Marinade: In a bowl, combine oil, garlic powder, ginger, soy sauce, rice vinegar, sesame oil, optional hot sauce, salt, and pepper.
3. In bowl add chicken. In a second bowl add broccoli and onions. Divide the marinade between the two bowls, stirring to coat each completely.
4. Air Fry: Add just the chicken to the air fryer basket/tray. Air Fry at 380°F/195°C for 10 minutes. Stir in the broccoli and onions with the chicken (make sure to include all the marinade). Continue to Air Fry at 380°F/195°C for 8-10 minutes, or until the chicken is cooked through. Make sure to stir halfway through cooking so broccoli gets cooked evenly.
5. Season with additional salt and pepper, to taste. Add fresh lemon juice on top (optional) and serve warm.
6. AIR FRYING OPTION #2: EXTRA CRISPY, CHARRED BROCCOLI
7. Combine chicken, broccoli and onion in bowl. Toss ingredients together.
8. Make Marinade: In a bowl, combine oil, garlic powder, ginger, soy sauce, rice vinegar, sesame oil, optional hot sauce, salt, and pepper. Add the chicken, broccoli and onions to the marinade. Stir thoroughly to combine the marinade with chicken, broccoli and onions.
9. Air Fry: Add ingredients to air fryer basket/tray. Air Fry 380°F/195°C for 16-20 minutes, shaking and gently tossing halfway through cooking. Make sure to toss so that everything cooks evenly. Check chicken to make sure it's cooked through. If not, cook for additional 3-5 minutes.
10. If needed, season with additional salt and pepper, to taste. Add fresh lemon juice on top (optional) and serve warm.

NOTES

Air Frying Tips and Notes:Shake or turn as directed in the recipe. Don't overcrowd the air fryer basket.Recipes were tested in 3.4 to 6 qt air fryers. If using a larger air fryer, the recipe might cook quicker so adjust cooking time.Remember to set a timer to shake/flip/toss as directed in recipe.

Air Fryer Chicken Legs

Servings: 4
Cooking Time: 18 Minutes

Ingredients:

- 8 to 10 bone-in, skin-on chicken legs/drumsticks (about 2 1/4 pounds)
- 1 tablespoon extra-virgin olive oil
- 1 tablespoon dark brown sugar
- 2 teaspoons smoked paprika
- 1 teaspoon kosher salt
- 1/2 teaspoon black pepper
- 1/2 teaspoon dry mustard powder
- 1/4 teaspoon ground cayenne pepper
- Chopped fresh cilantro or parsley or serving

Directions:

1. With paper towels, pat the chicken legs dry, and place in a large mixing bowl. Drizzle with the oil.
2. In a small bowl, stir together the brown sugar, smoked paprika, salt, pepper, mustard, and cayenne. Sprinkle over the chicken, then toss to evenly coat.
3. Preheat the air fryer to 400 degrees F, according to the manufacturer's instructions. Arrange a single layer of the drumsticks in the basket.
4. Air fry chicken legs for 10 minutes, then slide out the basket and flip the legs. Return to the air fryer and cook for 8 additional minutes, until the internal temperature of the chicken reaches at least 165 degrees F when a meat thermometer is inserted at the thickest part without touching the bone (I remove mine around 190 degrees F and it is still very juicy. The extra time ensures the skin is nice and crisp). Transfer to a plate and let rest 5 minutes. Serve hot, sprinkled with chopped cilantro or parsley as desired.

Notes

TO STORE: Refrigerate chicken in an airtight storage container for up to 4 days.

TO REHEAT: Gently rewarm leftovers on a baking sheet in the oven at 350 degrees F or in the microwave.

TO FREEZE: Freeze chicken in an airtight, freezer-safe storage container for up to 3 months. Let thaw overnight in the refrigerator before reheating.

Air Fryer Chicken Cordon Bleu

Servings: 4
Cooking Time: 20 Minutes

Ingredients:
- 4 small chicken breasts boneless skinless, 4-5 oz each
- salt and ground black pepper to taste
- ⅛ teaspoon dried thyme leaves
- 4 slices deli Swiss cheese
- 4 slices deli ham
- 1 egg beaten
- ⅓ cup panko bread crumbs
- ½ cup seasoned bread crumbs

Directions:
1. Place the chicken breast on a flat work surface and butterfly the chicken by cutting most of the way through so it opens like a book. Pound to ¼ " thickness.
2. Season chicken with salt, pepper, and thyme.
3. Place the ham and cheese inside each chicken breast. Close the breasts and secure with a toothpick.
4. Mix panko bread crumbs and seasoned bread crumbs in a shallow dish. Dip chicken into egg and then bread crumbs.
5. Preheat the air fryer to 370°F.
6. Generously spray the rolls with cooking spray and place in the bottom of the air fryer basket.
7. Cook 10 minutes. Flip chicken over and cook an additional 8-10 minutes or until bread crumbs are crisp and chicken reaches 165°F.

Air Fryer Chicken Katsu

Servings: 4
Cooking Time: 25 Minutes

Ingredients:
- 2 boneless skinless chicken breasts
- Kosher salt, to taste
- Black pepper, to taste
- 2 large eggs, beaten
- 1 tablespoon water
- 1 ½ cups Panko bread crumbs
- KATSU SAUCE
- 3 tablespoons ketchup
- 1 tablespoon Worcestershire sauce
- 1/2 tablespoon oyster sauce (or soy sauce), plus more to taste
- 2 teaspoons brown sugar
- SERVE WITH
- Steamed Rice
- Steamed Vegetables
- Katsu Sauce

Directions:
1. Dry the chicken breasts with paper towels, then use a sharp knife to cut them in half horizontally, creating four filets. If necessary, use a meat mallet to pound each portion to about ½-inch thickness. Season with salt and pepper, to taste.
2. Preheat the air fryer to 350 degrees F, spraying the inner basket with cooking spray.
3. In a wide, shallow bowl, whisk together the egg and water until well combined. To a second bowl, add the Panko bread crumbs.
4. Dredge the chicken in the egg, then press them into the bread crumbs, coating evenly. Repeat the process a second time with each piece, double coating them.
5. Place the chicken in an even layer in the air fryer basket, spraying the top with cooking spray.
6. Air fry for 16-18 minutes, carefully flipping the chicken halfway through and spraying with cooking spray before continuing to cook until golden brown and 165 degrees F internally. Repeat with the remaining pieces of chicken.
7. Transfer the katsu to a cutting board to rest for at least 5 minutes before slicing. Serve over rice, with vegetables and katsu sauce.

Air Fryer Popcorn Chicken With Jalapeño Ranch

Servings: 6
Cooking Time: 15 Minutes

Ingredients:
- 500 g (1lb) chicken breasts
- 1 cup flour
- 2 eggs beaten
- 2 cups panko breadcrumbs
- 1 tsp salt
- 1 tsp smoked paprika
- 1 tsp garlic powder
- 1 tsp dried oregano
- 1 tsp pepper
- For the Jalapeño Ranch
- ½ cup sour cream
- ½ cup mayonnaise
- 1 tbsp Jalapeños chopped
- 2 tsp dill finely chopped
- 1 tsp parsley finely chopped
- 2 tsp chives finely chopped
- 1-2 tsp lime juice
- salt and pepper to taste

Directions:
1. Slice the chicken into bite size chunks.
2. Place the flour, eggs and panko breadcrumbs in separate shallow bowls. Season the flour with salt and pepper. Season the breadcrumbs with the spices.
3. Coat the chicken in the flour, then in the beaten egg and finally in the breadcrumbs mixture. For a thicker coating, repeat the egg and breadcrumb steps.
4. Place the chicken pieces in a single layer in the basket of an air fryer then drizzle or spray with olive oil.
5. Cook the chicken at 200°C/390°F for 15 minutes, turning half way through.
6. Finely chop the herbs and place in a bowl. Mix in the mayonnaise, sour cream, lime juice, jalapeños, salt and pepper. Taste and adjust seasoning if necessary.
7. Remove the popcorn chicken from the air fryer then serve with the ranch and lime wedges.

Cauliflower Rice Arancini

Servings: 2
Cooking Time: 25 Minutes

Ingredients:
- 1 Italian chicken sausage link (casing removed (2 3/4 oz))
- 2 1/4 cups riced cauliflower (frozen works great)
- 1/4 teaspoon kosher salt
- 2 tablespoons homemade marinara (plus optional more for serving)
- 1/2 cup part skim shredded mozzarella
- 1 large egg (beaten)
- 1/4 cup bread crumbs* (or gluten-free crumbs)
- 1 tablespoon grated Pecorino Romano or parmesan*
- cooking spray

Directions:
1. Heat a medium skillet over medium-high heat. Add the sausage and cook, breaking the meat up with spoon as it cooks as small as you can, about 4 to 5 minutes.
2. Add the cauliflower, salt and marinara and cook 6 minutes on medium heat, stirring until the cauliflower is tender and heated through.
3. Remove from heat and add the mozzarella cheese to the skillet and stir well to mix. Let it cool 3 to 4 minutes, until it's easy to handle.
4. Spray a 1/4 cup measuring cup with cooking spray and fill with cauliflower mixture, leveling the top. Use a small spoon to scoop out into your palm and roll into a ball. Set aside on a dish.
5. Repeat with the remaining cauliflower, you should have 6 balls.
6. Place the egg in one bowl and the breadcrumbs in another.
7. Add the parmesan to the crumbs and mix.
8. Dip the ball in the egg, then in the crumbs and transfer to a baking sheet. Spray the top with cooking spray.
9. If baking in the oven, bake 425F 25 minutes, until golden. If making in the air fryer, bake 400F for 9 minutes turning halfway until golden.

10. Serve with marinara sauce, for dipping.
Notes
*half of the crumbs get tossed, the n.i. and smart points accounts for that.

Air Fryer Frozen Turkey Burgers
Servings: 4
Cooking Time: 15 Minutes

Ingredients:
- 4 frozen turkey burgers ½ inch thick
- 4 tablespoons barbecue sauce
- For Serving
- 4 hamburger buns
- lettuce, tomatoes, onions, mayonnaise optional

Directions:
1. Preheat air fryer to 375°F.
2. Place turkey burgers in a single layer in the air fryer basket.
3. Cook burgers for 13-14 minutes, flipping halfway through the cook time and brushing with bbq sauce.
4. Serve on hamburger buns with desired fixings.

Air Fryer Chicken Nuggets
Servings: 4
Cooking Time: 10 Minutes

Ingredients:
- 1 lb boneless skinless chicken breast
- 1/2 tsp salt
- 1/4 tsp pepper
- 1/4 cup flour
- 1/2 cup melted butter or 1 large egg
- 1/2 cup breadcrumbs
- 1/2 cup parmesan grated
- 1 tsp dried parsley
- olive oil spray
- Garnish:
- ketchup, bbq sauce, ranch dressing, or your favorite dipping sauce.

Directions:
1. Trim any excess fat from the chicken breast and cut the chicken into nugget-sized pieces. Season with salt and pepper.
2. Set out 3 shallow bowls. In the first bowl put the flour, in the second bowl put the melted butter or beaten egg.
3. In the third bowl, mix together the breadcrumbs, dried parsley, and parmesan cheese.
4. One at a time dip each piece of chicken in the flour first, then the butter or egg, and finally the breadcrumb mixture.
5. Once all nuggets are ready to cook, give them a light spray with olive oil and place them on a single layer in the air fryer. Cook for 7 minutes at 400F and then flip the nuggets. Cook for another 1 to 3 minutes at 400F until they are golden.
6. Serve with your favorite dipping sauce.
Notes
Make sure not to overcrowd the air fryer basket. The hot air needs to reach all the sides of the nuggets, so they crisp up.
Press the breadcrumbs onto the nuggets to help them adhere well. Doing so helps give the chicken a more even coating.
The key to cooking chicken nuggets in the air fryer perfectly is to ensure all the chicken nuggets are as uniformly as possible. You want them all to cook for the same amount of time.
After dipping the chicken nuggets, shake off any excess egg so the nuggets don't taste eggy.

Air Fryer Garlic-herb Turkey Breast
Servings: 6

Ingredients:
- 2 lb. turkey breast, skin on
- Kosher salt
- Freshly ground black pepper
- 4 tbsp. butter, melted
- 3 cloves garlic, minced
- 1 tsp. freshly chopped thyme
- 1 tsp. freshly chopped rosemary
- See All Nutritional Information

Directions:
1. Pat turkey breast dry and season on both sides with salt and pepper.
2. In a small bowl, combine melted butter, garlic, thyme, and rosemary. Brush butter all over turkey breast.

3. Place in basket of air fryer, skin side up and cook at 375° for 40 minutes or until internal temperature reaches 160°, flipping halfway through.
4. Let rest for 5 minutes before slicing.

Air Fryer Chicken Strips
Servings: 8
Cooking Time: 12 Minutes

Ingredients:
- 1 1/2 lbs chicken breast skinless and boneless
- 2 cups all purpose flour I used half whole wheat
- 2 large eggs
- 2 cups panko bread crumbs
- 1/2 teaspoon salt
- 1/2 teaspoon pepper
- 1 teaspoon dehydrated garlic optional
- 1 tablespoon butter melted

Directions:
1. Preheat the air fryer to 200C/400F.
2. Pat dry the chicken breast and slice them into 2-inch strips.
3. In one bowl, add the flour, in another bowl, add the eggs, and in the third bowl, add the panko bread crumbs, salt, pepper, and garlic.
4. Moving quickly, dip the chicken in the flour, then the egg mix, then the panko mix. Shake off any excess.
5. Add the chicken strips to the greased air fryer basket. Brush the exterior of the chicken with some butter and air fry for 12 minutes, flipping halfway through.
6. Once the chicken is cooked, remove it from the air fryer and serve immediately.

Notes
TO STORE: Leftovers can be stored in the refrigerator, covered, for up to five days.
TO FREEZE: Place the cooked and cooked breast strips in a shallow container and store them in the freezer for up to 6 months.
TO REHEAT: Either reheat back in the air fryer or a preheated oven. Avoid reheating in the microwave as the chicken will lose its crispiness.

Air Fryer Grilled Chicken Tenders
Servings: 4
Cooking Time: 10 Minutes

Ingredients:
- 10 chicken tenders
- 1 Tablespoon olive oil
- 1 teaspoon ground black pepper
- 1/2 teaspoon garlic powder
- 1/2 teaspoon onion powder
- 1/2 teaspoon paprika

Directions:
1. Preheat the Air Fryer to 400°F for 5 minutes. Prepare the Air Fryer basket with nonstick cooking spray or olive oil spray.
2. Using a cutting board, remove the tendon from the raw chicken tenders and add them to a medium-sized bowl.
3. Add the olive oil to the chicken tenders and toss them so that they are fully coated.
4. Add the seasonings to the chicken tenders and coat them.
5. Place the seasoned chicken in a single layer in the air fryer basket. Cook at 400°F for 10 minutes, flipping the chicken at the 5-minute mark. The chicken strips should be perfectly crispy and golden brown.
6. Use a meat thermometer to make sure the internal temperature reaches 165° degrees F. If not, cook for additional minutes until ready.
7. Serve the cooked chicken with your favorite dipping sauces, such as BBQ sauce, buffalo sauce, or honey mustard sauce.

NOTES
It doesn't take long to cook these grilled chicken tenders in the air fryer with no breading. You should only need 15 minutes to have the most delicious and flavorful grilled chicken tenders.
To make your chicken tenders crispy, make sure you only use the recommended amount of oil or cooking spray. Using too much oil can make your chicken tenders greasy, and they won't crisp up.
You can store these easy chicken tenders in an airtight container for 3-4 days!

Air Fryer Bacon Wrapped Chicken Bites

Servings: 4
Cooking Time: 10 Minutes

Ingredients:
- 1 pound boneless, skinless chicken breast
- 1 teaspoon olive oil
- 1/4 teaspoon smoked paprika
- 1/4 teaspoon garlic powder
- 1 Tablespoon brown sugar
- 6 slices bacon
- 2 Tablespoons Barbecue sauce

Directions:
1. Preheat the air fryer to 390 degrees Fahrenheit. Prepare the air fryer basket with nonstick cooking oil if needed.
2. Cut the raw chicken breasts into bite sized pieces.
3. Add the paprika, brown sugar, and garlic powder in a small bowl and mix until combined. Set aside.
4. Coat the chicken bites in olive oil and then toss the chicken pieces in the brown sugar mixture.
5. Take each slice of bacon and cut the bacon strips in half to fit the chicken bites.
6. Wrap each of the seasoned chicken bites with a piece of bacon.
7. Place each bacon wrapped piece of chicken in a single layer in the air fryer basket. Cook at 390 degrees Fahrenheit for 8-9 minutes, or until you have crispy bacon and the internal temperature has reached 165 degrees Fahrenheit.
8. Carefully remove the chicken bites from the Air Fryer and serve with your favorite dipping sauce such as barbecue sauce.

NOTES:If you don't have boneless skinless chicken breasts, consider using boneless skinless chicken thighs, chicken strips, or chicken tenderloins.
How do I store leftover bacon chicken bites?
Store leftover bacon wrapped chicken bites in an airtight container in the refrigerator for up to 3 days. To reheat, place the bacon wrapped chicken bites back into the air fryer and cook at 390 degrees Fahrenheit for 2-3 minutes or until heated through.

15 Minute Air Fryer Low Carb Chicken Enchiladas

Servings: 4
Cooking Time: 5 Minutes

Ingredients:
- 1 cup onion chopped
- 1 cup chicken stock
- 1 ½ tablespoons chili powder
- 2 teaspoons ground cumin
- ¾ teaspoon garlic powder
- ½ teaspoon crushed red pepper
- ¼ teaspoon salt
- 1 cup salsa can use tomato sauce
- 3 cups shredded skinless boneless rotisserie chicken breast
- 15 ounces can black beans rinsed and drained
- 12 6-inch carb-conscious tortillas
- 1 cup cheese shredded
- 1 cup tomato chopped
- ¼ cup fresh cilantro chopped
- 6 tablespoons sour cream

Directions:
1. Preheat Vortex Air Fryer to 350°F.
2. Combine the first 9 ingredients in a medium saucepan. Cook on medium heat for 2 minutes or until thickened.
3. Reserve 1 ½ cups sauce mixture. Add chicken and beans to pan; cook 2 minutes or until chicken is thoroughly heated.
4. Stack tortillas; wrap the stack in damp paper towels and microwave at HIGH for 25 seconds. Top with reserved sauce and cheese.
5. Spoon about ⅓ cup chicken mixture in center of each tortilla; roll-up. Arrange tortillas, seam sides down, in the bottom of a 13 x 9-inch glass or ceramic baking dish coated with cooking spray.
6. Broil 3 minutes or until cheese is lightly browned and sauce is bubbly. Top with tomato and cilantro. Serve with sour cream.

FISH & SEAFOOD RECIPES

Air Fryer Keto Coconut Shrimp
Servings: 8
Cooking Time: 10 Minutes

Ingredients:
- 25 large shrimp peeled and deveined
- 1/2 cup coconut flour
- 1 3/4 cup coconut flakes unsweetened
- 3 eggs
- 1 tbsp ground black pepper
- 1 tsp smoked paprika
- 1 tsp salt

Directions:
1. Preheat the Air Fryer to 390 degrees Fahrenheit. Prepare the air fryer basket with non stick cooking spray.
2. Arrange three bowls. Add the coconut flour, paprika, salt and pepper to one bowl. Coconut flakes to the second bowl, and beaten eggs in the third bowl.
3. Dip the shrimp into the coconut flour mixture, then dip into the egg mixture, and finally into the coconut flakes. Set aside on a wire rack until you've finished with all of the shrimp.
4. Add the coconut shrimp in a single layer into the prepared air fryer basket and cook for 8-10 minutes at 380 degrees Fahrenheit. Flip the shrimp halfway through.
5. Remove when golden brown and serve immediately.

NOTES
If you have any "hanging" coconut flakes they will likely brown faster than the shrimp. Air fryers also cook differently and have different wattages. You may need to add or take away time for this recipe depending on the type of air fryer you own.

Air Fryer Shrimp Fajitas
Servings: 4
Cooking Time: 8 Minutes

Ingredients:
- 1 lb shrimp fresh shrimp, peeled, tails off, deveined
- 1 medium red bell pepper
- 1 medium orange bell pepper
- 1 medium green bell pepper
- 1 medium yellow onion medium
- 2 tbsp fajita seasoning mix
- Toppings:
- 1 small avocado sliced
- 1 teaspoon cilantro fresh, chopped

Directions:
1. Cut the onion and bell peppers into strips and place them in a medium bowl.
2. Rinse the shrimp under water in a colander and then place on a paper towel to pat dry. Add to the bowl with the shrimp.
3. Add the fajita seasoning to the shrimp and bell peppers and toss to coat them evenly.
4. Add the shrimp, peppers, and onion to the basket of the air fryer.
5. Air fry the shrimp and vegetables at 400 degrees Fahrenheit for 8 minutes, tossing the mixture halfway through the cooking process.
6. Carefully remove from the air fryer and serve on a flour tortilla and top with your favorite toppings.

NOTES
This easy air fryer shrimp recipe can be served any way that you want. You can add the ingredients to a large bowl and top it with sour cream, cayenne pepper, and more. It's simple to turn this dish into air fryer shrimp fajita bowls. You can also get flour tortillas or corn tortillas and fill them fully! Perfect for busy weeknights. The best way to serve this recipe is to let everyone add their own toppings and enjoy.

Air Fryer Fish Tacos
Servings: 3
Cooking Time: 6 Minutes

Ingredients:
- 1 teaspoon garlic powder
- 1 teaspoon chili powder
- 1 teaspoon cumin
- 1/2 teaspoon kosher salt
- 1 cup Panko breadcrumbs
- 1 large egg

- 1 pound fresh cod filets cut in strips or pieces
- 8 small flour or corn tortillas
- Spicy Cream Sauce
- 1/2 cup mayonnaise
- 1/4 cup sriracha sauce
- 1 teaspoon fresh lime juice
- Optional Toppings
- 1 cup purple cabbage shredded
- 1 medium avocado sliced
- 1 cup cotija cheese crumbled
- 1 bunch cilantro garnish

Directions:

1. To prepare the air fryer basket, lightly spray with nonstick cooking spray, then set aside.
2. In a shallow medium bowl, add the garlic powder, chili powder, cumin, salt, and panko breadcrumbs. Stir together until well combined
3. In another shallow bowl, whisk egg. Dip each filet in the whisked egg, and then into the panko breadcrumb mixture. Be sure to coat both sides well.
4. Place filets in a single layer in the prepared air fryer basket and air fry at 350 degrees F for 6-7 minutes until golden brown.

NOTES

Top Tips

I use thinner fish for this recipe. Add a few extra minutes to cooking time if using thicker fish filets.

To confirm doneness, use a fork to flake tilapia fish fillet to see if it easily flakes. To confirm proper temperature, use a meat thermometer to confirm doneness. It should be 130-135 degrees F.

I use fresh tilapia fillets for this simple recipe, but you can use frozen fish fillets as well. Add an additional 2-3 minutes to cooking process.

Air-fried Beer Battered Fish Tacos With Mango Salsa Recipe

Ingredients:
- For the fish:
- 2 eggs
- 10 ounces of Mexican beer
- 1 1/2 cups of corn starch
- 1 1/2 cups of flour
- 1/2 tablespoon of chili powder
- 1 tablespoon of cumin
- Kosher salt and fresh cracked pepper to taste
- 1 pound of cod cut into large pieces
- Non-stick spray
- For the Salsa & to make the Taco:
- 3 peeled and medium-diced mangos
- 1/2 peeled, seeded and small diced red bell pepper
- 1 peeled, seeded and small diced jalapeno
- 1/2 peeled and small diced red onion
- 1 tablespoon of chopped fresh cilantro
- Juice of 1 lime
- Kosher salt and fresh cracked pepper to taste
- 1/2 thinly sliced head of red cabbage
- Soft corn tortillas
- Crumbled queso fresco for garnish
- Sliced green onions and cilantro leaves for garnish

Directions:

1. For the salsa:
2. Combine the mangos, peppers, onion, chopped cilantro, lime juice together in a medium size bowl and mix. Refrigerate until ready to serve.
3. For the fish:
4. In a medium size bowl whisk together the eggs and beer and set aside.
5. In a separate medium bowl whisk together the cornstarch, flour, chili powder, cumin, salt and pepper.
6. Coat the fish in the egg-beer mixture and transfer it to the flour mixture and dredge to completely coat on all sides.
7. Spray the bottom of the air fryer basket with no-stick spray and place in the fish and spray the tops of the fish with no-stick spray.
8. Cook at 375 degrees for 15 minutes
9. Place the air fried fish on a corn tortilla and top off with cabbage, salsa, queso fresco, green onions, and cilantro.
10. Enjoy!

Air Fryer Salmon With Maple Soy Glaze

Servings: 4
Cooking Time: 8 Minutes

Ingredients:
- 3 tbsp pure maple syrup
- 3 tbsp reduced sodium soy sauce (or gluten-free soy sauce)
- 1 tbsp sriracha hot sauce
- 1 clove garlic (smashed)
- 4 wild salmon fillets (skinless (6 oz each))

Directions:
1. Combine maple syrup, soy sauce, sriracha and garlic in a small bowl, pour into a gallon sized resealable bag and add the salmon.
2. Marinate 20 to 30 minutes, turning once in a while.
3. Lightly spray the basket with oil.
4. Remove the fish from the marinade, reserving and pat dry with paper towels.
5. Place the fish in the air fryer, in batches, air fry 400F 7 to 8 minutes, or longer depending on thickness of the salmon.
6. Meanwhile, pour the marinade in a small saucepan and bring to a simmer over medium-low heat and reduce until it thickens into a glaze, 1 to 2 minutes. Spoon over salmon just before eating.

Air Fryer Bacon Wrapped Scallops

Servings: 4
Cooking Time: 13 Minutes

Ingredients:
- 16 large sea scallops cleaned & pat dry with paper towels
- 8 slices center cut bacon
- 1/4 cup Williamson Bros. BBQ sauce

Directions:
1. Slice bacon in half and place the bacon in the air fryer to partially cook at 400 for 3 minutes.
2. 16 large sea scallops
3. Pat the scallops dry with paper towels to remove any moisture.
4. Wrap each scallop in 1/2 slice of bacon and secure it with a toothpick.
5. 8 slices center cut bacon
6. Place scallops in air fryer (I can fit 8 at a time in my basket style air fryer)
7. Lightly brush scallop with your favorite barbecue sauce. I recommend a thinner sauce – not a heavy thick sauce. You can also just spray with olive oil and salt/pepper.
8. Cook at 400 for 5 minutes. Turn scallops delicately and baste again with bbq sauce. Cook for another 5 minutes at 400 until scallop is tender and opaque and bacon is cooked through. Serve hot.
9. 1/4 cup Williamson Bros. BBQ sauce
10. I also sprinkled a little Historic BBQ Red seasoning on them when they were done.

Crisp-skinned Air Fryer Salmon With Salsa Verde

Servings: 4
Cooking Time: 25 Minutes

Ingredients:
- 4 x 185g salmon fillets, skin on
- 1 tablespoon extra virgin olive oil
- 2 teaspoon sea salt flakes
- 1 small shallot, chopped finely
- 1 clove garlic, crushed
- 2 teaspoon finely grated lemon rind
- 2 tablespoon lemon juice
- 2 tablespoon finely chopped dill
- ¼ cup chopped flat-leaf parsley
- 2 tablespoon chopped chives
- 1 tablespoon baby capers, chopped coarsely
- to serve: extra sea salt flakes

Directions:
1. Preheat a 7-litre air fryer to 200°C/400°F for 3 minutes.
2. Rub salmon with oil, then sprinkle with salt flakes.
3. Taking care, line the air fryer basket with a silicone mat, if available. Place salmon, skin-side up, in the basket; at 200°C/400°F, cook for 8 minutes until skin is crisp and salmon is cooked to your liking.

4. Meanwhile, to make salsa verde, combine remaining ingredients in a medium bowl; mix well. Season.
5. Serve salmon topped with salsa verde and sprinkled with extra salt flakes.

Air Fryer Coconut Shrimp
Servings: 4

Ingredients:
- FOR THE SHRIMP
- 1/2 c. all-purpose flour
- Kosher salt
- Freshly ground black pepper
- 1 c. panko bread crumbs
- 1/2 c. shredded sweetened coconut
- 2 large eggs, beaten
- 1 lb. large tail-on shrimp, peeled and deveined
- 1/2 c. mayonnaise
- 1 tbsp. sriracha
- 1 tbsp. Thai sweet chili sauce

Directions:
1. In a shallow bowl, season flour with salt and black pepper. In another shallow bowl, combine panko and coconut. In a third shallow bowl, beat eggs to blend.
2. Working one at a time, dip shrimp into seasoned flour, shaking off any excess. Dip into eggs, then into panko mixture, gently pressing to adhere.
3. Working in batches if necessary, in an air-fryer basket, arrange shrimp in a single layer. Cook at 400° until shrimp is golden brown and cooked through, 7 to 9 minutes.
4. In a small bowl, combine mayonnaise, sriracha, and chili sauce.
5. Arrange shrimp on a platter. Serve with dipping sauce alongside.

Air Fryer Salmon In 6 Minutes Tender And Flaky
Servings: 4
Cooking Time: 6 Minutes

Ingredients:
- 4 fillets salmon 6 oz each
- 1 tablespoon olive oil
- 1/2 teaspoon salt
- 1/2 teaspoon pepper
- 2 tablespoons brown sugar
- 1/2 teaspoon smoked paprika
- 1/2 teaspoon garlic powder
- 1/2 teaspoon onion powder

Directions:
1. In a small bowl, coat the salmon with oil, then add the salt and pepper.
2. Mix the remaining sugar and spices and rub over the salmon.
3. Add the salmon skin side down to the air fryer basket and air fry at 200C/400F for 6 minutes, or until cooked.
4. Remove from the air fryer basket and sprinkle with chopped parsley.

Notes

TO STORE: Leftovers can be stored in an airtight container in the refrigerator for up to 3 days.

TO FREEZE: Place the cooked and cooled salmon in a ziplock bag and store it in the freezer for up to two months.

TO REHEAT: Heat the leftovers gently in a skillet or pan on the stovetop over medium heat until hot.

Air Fryer Lobster Tail
Servings: 4
Cooking Time: 5 Minutes

Ingredients:
- 4 5-oz Lobster tails
- 1/4 cup Salted butter (melted; 1/2 stick)
- 2 cloves Garlic (crushed)
- 2 tsp Lemon juice
- 1/2 tsp Smoked paprika
- 1 pinch Cayenne pepper (or more if you want extra heat)

Directions:
1. If tails are frozen, thaw them overnight in the fridge, or in a bag submerged in cold water on the counter for about 30 minutes.
2. Preheat the air fryer to 400 degrees F (204 degrees C)for a few minutes.
3. Butterfly the lobster tails. Using kitchen shears, cut down the center of the shell lengthwise, starting from the end opposite

the tail fins, continuing down until you reach the tail but without cutting the tail. You want to cut through the top of the shell, but don't cut through the bottom shell. Use your thumbs and fingers to spread open the shell on top, then use your thumbs and fingers to spread open the shell. Run a bamboo skewer through the center of the flesh lengthwise to prevent curling.

4. In a small bowl, whisk together the melted butter, garlic, lemon juice, smoked paprika, and cayenne. Brush the butter mixture over the lobster meat.

5. Cook lobster tails in the air fryer for 5-6 minutes for 5-ounce lobster tails, or until the meat is opaque and internal temperature in the thickest part reaches 140 degrees F (60 degrees C). (If your tails are a different size, a good rule of thumb for lobster tail air fryer time is about 1 minute per ounce of individual tail. For example, if your lobster tails are 8 ounces each, you'll air fry them for about 8 minutes.) After cooking for 1 minute per ounce of individual tail, check the internal temperature with a meat thermometer and if they are not done yet, cook for 1-3 more minutes as needed.

Air Fryer Breaded Shrimp

Servings: 4
Cooking Time: 8 Minutes

Ingredients:
- 1 pound large raw shrimp peeled and deveined (I use 31/40 size)
- 1 cup Italian Breadcrumbs
- ¼ cup grated Parmesan cheese
- 1/2 cup all purpose flour
- 1/3 cup water
- 1/2 tsp dried parsley flakes
- 1/2 tsp paprika
- ½ tsp salt
- ¼ tsp ground black pepper
- 1 large egg

Directions:
1. In a shallow bowl, add breadcrumbs, parmesan cheese, parsley flakes, paprika, salt and pepper. Stir with a fork to combine ingredients.

2. In another large bowl, add the flour, egg, and water. Stir together to make a liquid batter.

3. Toss shrimp with the flour and egg batter, until they are coated on both sides.

4. Dredge each piece of shrimp in the panko mixture, coating both sides.

5. Lightly spray the air fryer basket, and place each shrimp into the basket, without stacking or overlapping.

6. Lightly spritz the coated shrimp with olive oil and then place shrimp in the air fryer basket. Air Fry at 380 degrees F for 8-10 minutes, flipping shrimp halfway through air frying.

NOTES

Variations

Use panko breadcrumbs - Instead of using regular bread crumbs, you can use Panko bread crumbs.

Change the seasoning - Use Old Bay seasoning, lemon pepper, red pepper flakes, Cajun seasoning, and any other flavors that you want to add to this shrimp recipe. The flavors take to the larger shrimp easily.

Make air fryer frozen shrimp - If you want to cook tender seafood, you can cook frozen shrimp in the air fryer as well. Just add them in a single layer in the basket of the air fryer.

Air-fryer Fish Tacos

Servings: 4

Ingredients:
- 2 cups shredded green cabbage
- ¼ cup coarsely chopped fresh cilantro
- 1 scallion, thinly sliced
- 5 tablespoons lime juice (from 2 limes), divided
- 1 tablespoon avocado oil
- 1 large avocado
- 2 tablespoons sour cream
- 1 small clove garlic, grated
- ¼ teaspoon salt
- 1 large egg white
- ⅓ cup dry whole-wheat breadcrumbs

- 1 tablespoon chili powder
- 1 pound skinless mahi-mahi fillets, cut into 2- to 3-inch strips
- Avocado oil cooking spray
- 8 (6 inch) corn tortillas, warmed
- 1 medium tomato, chopped

Directions:
1. Toss cabbage, cilantro, scallion, 2 tablespoons lime juice and avocado oil together in a medium bowl; set aside.
2. Cut avocado in half lengthwise; using a spoon, scoop the pulp into the bowl of a mini food processor. Add sour cream, garlic, salt and the remaining 3 tablespoons lime juice; process until smooth, about 30 seconds. (Alternatively, mash with a fork to reach desired consistency.) Set aside.
3. Preheat air fryer to 400°F. Place egg white in a shallow dish; whisk until frothy. Combine breadcrumbs and chili powder in a separate shallow dish. Pat fish dry with a paper towel. Coat the fish with egg white, letting excess drip off; dredge in the breadcrumb mixture, pressing to adhere.
4. Working in batches if needed, arrange the fish in an even layer in the fryer basket; coat the fish well with cooking spray. Cook until crispy and golden on one side, about 3 minutes. Flip the fish; coat with cooking spray and cook until it's crispy and flakes easily, about 3 minutes. Flake the fish into bite-size pieces. Top each tortilla evenly with fish, avocado crema (about 1 tablespoon each), cabbage slaw (about 1/4 cup each) and tomato. Serve with lime wedges, if desired.

Air Fryer Oven Cheesy Scalloped Potatoes

Ingredients:
- 3 tablespoons butter
- 1 small white or yellow onion, peeled and thinly sliced
- 4 large garlic cloves, minced
- 1/4 cup all-purpose flour
- 1 cup chicken stock or vegetable stock
- 2 cups milk (2% or whole milk, recommended)
- 1 1/2 teaspoons Kosher salt
- 1/2 teaspoon black pepper
- 2 teaspoons fresh thyme leaves, divided
- 10 Yukon Gold Potatoes, sliced into 1/8-inch rounds
- 2 cups freshly-grated sharp cheddar cheese*, divided
- 1/2 cup freshly-grated Parmesan cheese, plus extra for serving

Directions:
1. Prep oven and baking dish: Pre-heat air fryer to 400°F. Grease a 8 x 8-inch baking dish with cooking spray, and set it aside.
2. Sauté the onion and garlic. Melt butter in a large sauté pan over medium-high heat. Add onion, and sauté for 4-5 minutes until soft and translucent. Add garlic and sauté for an additional 1-2 minutes until fragrant. Stir in the flour until it is evenly combined, and cook for 1 more minute.
3. Simmer the sauce. Gradually pour in the stock, and whisk until combined. Add in the milk, salt, pepper, and 1 teaspoon thyme, and whisk until combined. Continue cooking for an additional 1-2 minutes until the sauce just barely begins to simmer around the edges of the pan and thickens. Then remove from heat and set aside.
4. Layer the potatoes. Spread half of the sliced potatoes in an even layer on the bottom of the pan. Top evenly with half of the cream sauce. Then sprinkle evenly with 1 cup of the shredded cheddar cheese, and all of the Parmesan cheese. Top evenly with the remaining sliced potatoes, the other half of the cream sauce, and the remaining 1 cup of cheddar cheese.
5. Bake: Cover the pan with aluminum foil and bake at 400 degrees for 40 minutes. The sauce should be nice and bubbly around the edges. Then remove the foil and bake uncovered for 10-15 minutes, or until the potatoes are cooked through.

6. Cool. Transfer the pan to a cooling rack, and sprinkle with the remaining teaspoon of thyme and extra Parmesan.
7. Serve. Serve warm.

Air Fryer Fish & Chips

Servings: 2
Cooking Time: 25 Minutes

Ingredients:
- Chips:
- 2 large potatoes, scrubbed, dried & sliced into chunky chips
- 1 Tbsp olive oil
- Salt, to taste
- Fish:
- 2 x 200g kingklip fillets (or similar firm white fish)
- 1 cup flour
- 1 XL egg, whisked
- ½ cup panko breadcrumbs
- ½ tsp sweet paprika
- ½ tsp garlic powder
- Salt and pepper, to taste
- Tartar sauce:
- 200ml mayonnaise
- 3 Tbsp baby capers, roughly chopped
- 3 Tbsp gherkins, finely minced
- 2 Tbsp fresh parsley, finely minced
- 1 Tbsp lemon zest
- 1 Tbsp lemon juice
- Lemon wedges, to serve

Directions:
1. In a bowl combine the potatoes, olive oil and salt.
2. Toss well to coat.
3. Spread out on one of the slotted Vortex Oven baking trays.
4. Set the Vortex Oven to Air Fry for 10 min at 202°C.
5. Once preheated add the chips in the bottom half of the oven, above the solid baking tray.
6. Place flour and whisked egg in 2 shallow bowls.
7. In a third shallow bowl combine the panko breadcrumbs, paprika, garlic powder and a little salt and pepper. Mix.
8. Season the fish fillets with salt and pepper.

9. Dip each piece in flour, shake off any excess, followed by egg and then the seasoned breadcrumbs.
10. Place the fish pieces onto a slotted Vortex Oven baking tray, allowing room in between each piece for proper air circulation.
11. Once the chips have finished their initial 10 minutes, immediately add the fish to the upper half of the oven. Set the Vortex Oven to Air Fry for another 10 min at 202°C. Turn halfway through.
12. While the fish is cooking combine the mayonnaise, capers, gherkins, parsley, lemon zest and lemon juice in a bowl. Mix well.
13. Serve fish and chips fresh out of the oven with a dollop of tartar sauce and a generous squeeze of lemon.

Cajun Air Fryer Fish

Ingredients:
- Fresh fish fillets. Use any sustainable white fish. I used hake but halibut, cod, tilapia, bass, grouper, haddock, snapper or catfish will all work well.
- Olive oil - Vegetable oil like avocado oil is a good substitution
- Cajun seasoning/Cajun spice. Most supermarkets will have a cajun spice blend in their spice aisle.
- Smoked paprika
- Garlic powder. Onion powder can also be used
- Fresh lemon juice

Directions:
1. Slice the fish into portions then place in the air fryer basket. In a small bowl, mix the olive oil, lemon juice and seasonings together then spoon over the fish. I don't usually add parchment paper to the basket but you can if you're worried about the fish sticking. You can also spray the basket with cooking spray or olive oil. Air fry for 8-10 minutes at 200°C/400°F until the fish is caramelized on the outside and opaque and juicy on the inside. Cooking time will depend on the thickness of the fish but

generally fish is cooked when it flakes apart easily and a fork can be inserted without any resistance. Remove from the air fryer then serve with lemon wedges.

Air Fryer Blackened Mahi Mahi
Servings: 4
Cooking Time: 9 Minutes

Ingredients:
- 4 mahi mahi fillets 3-4 oz each
- 2 tablespoons olive oil
- 3 tablespoons blackening seasoning

Directions:
1. Preheat air fryer to 400°F.
2. Pat fillets dry and generously rub with olive oil then coat them with blackening seasoning.
3. Place fillets in the air fryer basket and cook for 7-9 minutes.
4. Fish should reach 145°F internally and be opaque and flaky.

Notes
For the best crispy crust, preheat the air fryer first. If cooking in batches, keep warm in the oven and broil before serving.
Cooking time can vary with the thickness of the fish. Check the temperature of the fish early to ensure it doesn't overcook.
Serving Suggestion: Serve with fruit salsa like pineapple salsa or the quick bell pepper salsa below.
Quick Bell Pepper Salsa (optional): Dice one Roma tomato, half a bell pepper, and two tablespoons of red onion. Season with a squeeze of lime juice, a teaspoon of olive oil, and salt and pepper. Add a sprinkle of cilantro.

Air Fryer Mahi Mahi
Servings: 3-4
Cooking Time: 12 Minutes

Ingredients:
- 1 to 1 1/2 pounds mahi mahi fillets
- 2 tablespoons olive oil
- 2 cups panko breadcrumbs
- 1 teaspoon paprika
- 1/2 teaspoon garlic powder
- 1/2 teaspoon onion powder
- 1/2 teaspoon salt
- 1/2 teaspoon pepper
- OPTIONAL
- Lemon wedges, for serving

Directions:
1. Preheat your air fryer to 400 degrees.
2. Place the mahi mahi fillets on a large plate and drizzle or baste with olive oil.
3. In a shallow dish, mix the panko breadcrumbs, paprika, garlic powder, onion powder, salt, and pepper.
4. Dip each mahi mahi fillet into the panko mixture then place in a single layer in the air fryer basket. Spritz with cooking oil.
5. Cook for 12 to 15 minutes, flipping the mahi mahi halfway through cooking.
6. Remove them from the air fryer, serve with lemon wedges, and enjoy!

NOTES
HOW TO REHEAT MAHI MAHI IN THE AIR FRYER
Preheat your air fryer to 350 degrees.
Place the leftover mahi mahi in the air fryer and cook for about 3 to 4 minutes until heated thoroughly.
HOW TO COOK FROZEN MAHI MAHI IN THE AIR FRYER
Preheat your air fryer to 400 degrees.
Place the fillets in a single layer and cook for 13 to 14 minutes until heated thoroughly. Flip the mahi mahi halfway through cooking. If the fish is breaded, spritz with oil once at the beginning and once halfway through.

Air Fryer Cod
Servings: 4
Cooking Time: 10 Minutes

Ingredients:
- 4 125g Fresh Cod loins: you can substitute for fillets too
- 30 g melted unsalted butter
- 1 Lemon sliced
- Salt to taste
- black pepper to taste

Directions:
1. Preheat the air fryer at 200C/400F for 5 minutes.

2. Pat the cod fillets dry so it is moist-free. Season the fish generously with salt and black pepper then brush the melted butter on one side of the fish
3. Spray the air fryer basket with cooking oil. Place the cod fillet/loin in the air fryer basket buttered side down making sure they are not touching. Brush the remaining butter on top of the fish, add one lemon slice each to the fish
4. Cook for 10 minutes, carefully remove the fish and transfer to a plate. Serve with lemon butter sauce, roasted potatoes and veggies and enjoy!

NOTES

Check on the cod earlier than the time specified for this recipe so as not to overcook the fish. Remember, the thickness of your fish would determine how long it cooks in an air fryer. see the timing on this recipe as a guide. A good starting point to start checking on the fish is from 6 minutes.

As with the majority of air fryer recipes, do not overcrowd the air fryer basket so as to allow the food to cook evenly.

Customise the seasoning to taste.

Let the cod come to room temperature a few minutes before you cook for accurate cooking. The temperature of cooked fish should register at 145F/62C.

Do not leave the fish in the air fryer once the cooking is completed otherwise the fish would overcook and maybe even dry out.

Don't own an air fryer but would like to try this recipe, bake in the oven @200C/400F for 10 minutes. You can also cook your fresh or frozen cod in an air fryer in under 3 minutes.

Air Fryer Fried Shrimp

Servings: 4

Ingredients:
- Deselect All
- Fried Shrimp:
- 1 pound large shrimp (16/20 count), peeled and deveined, tails on
- Kosher salt and freshly ground black pepper
- 1/2 cup all-purpose flour
- 2 large eggs
- 1 cup panko breadcrumbs
- Nonstick cooking spray, for the shrimp
- Spicy Remoulade Sauce:
- 1/2 cup mayonnaise
- 2 tablespoons chopped pickled jalapenos
- 2 tablespoons whole grain mustard
- 1 tablespoon ketchup
- 1 tablespoon hot sauce
- 1 scallion, thinly sliced

Directions:
1. For the fried shrimp: Pat the shrimp dry between a couple paper towels, then season with a pinch of salt and a few grinds of pepper.
2. Whisk the flour with 3/4 teaspoon salt and few grinds of pepper in a shallow bowl or baking dish. Whisk the eggs with a pinch of salt in another shallow bowl. Add the panko to a third shallow bowl. Dip a shrimp in the seasoned flour, shaking off any excess, then dip in the beaten eggs. Dredge in the panko, turning until evenly coated. Transfer to a large plate or a rimmed baking sheet and repeat with the remaining shrimp.
3. Preheat a 5 quart air fryer to 385 degrees F. Working in batches, place some of the shrimp in a single layer in the fryer basket, then spray lightly with cooking spray. Cook, flipping halfway through, until the shrimp are golden brown and cooked through, about 10 minutes.
4. For the spicy remoulade sauce: Meanwhile, stir together the mayonnaise, pickled jalapenos, mustard, ketchup, hot sauce and scallion in a small bowl until smooth. Serve with the fried shrimp for dipping.

Cook's Note

You may need to fry the shrimp in 2 to 3 batches, depending on the size of your air-fryer basket.

Air Fryer Scallops

Servings: 4
Cooking Time: 5 Minutes

Ingredients:

- 1/2 lb scallops
- 1/2 teaspoon salt
- 1/4 teaspoon pepper
- 2 tablespoons butter divided
- 1/4 cup parsley finely chopped
- 1/2 small lemon sliced

Directions:

1. Pat dry the scallops and then sprinkle with salt and pepper. Brush one tablespoon of butter over the scallops.
2. Generously grease an air fryer basket with cooking spray and add a single layer of scallops.
3. Air fry at 200C/400 for 5-7 minutes, flipping halfway through.
4. Remove them from the air fryer basket, and brush more butter on them. Sprinkle with finely chopped parsley and serve with sliced lemon.
5. Notes
6. TO STORE: Place leftover scallops in a shallow container and store them in the refrigerator for up to two days.
7. TO FREEZE: Once the scallops have cooled to room temperature, place them in a shallow container and store them in the freezer for up to two months.
8. TO REHEAT: Reheat in the air fryer or microwave until warm.

Air Fryer Shrimp

Servings: 4
Cooking Time: 7 Minutes

Ingredients:

- 1 lb shrimp large or extra large
- 1 tablespoon olive oil
- 1/2 tablespoon lemon juice
- 1/2 teaspoon salt
- 1/2 teaspoon pepper
- 1/2 teaspoon garlic
- 1/2 teaspoon smoked paprika
- 1 teaspoon Italian seasonings

Directions:

1. Pat dry shrimp with a paper towel.
2. In a mixing bowl, whisk together the olive oil and lemon juice. Add the seasonings and mix well. Toss through the shrimp in the seasoning mix.
3. Cook the shrimp at 200C/400F for 7-8 minutes.
4. Serve immediately.
5. Notes
6. TO STORE: Air fryer shrimp can be stored in the refrigerator for up to 3 days in an air-tight container.
7. TO FREEZE: Place leftovers in a ziplock bag and store it in the freezer for up to 2 months.
8. TO REHEAT: Thaw and then put on the baking sheet or in the air fryer basket to reheat until crispy.

Air Fryer Salmon And Swiss Chard

Servings: 4

Ingredients:

- 1 medium red onion (sliced 1/2 inch thick)
- 1 1/2 tbsp. oil, divided
- Kosher salt and pepper
- 1 large bunch red Swiss chard (thick stems discarded, leaves chopped)
- 2 cloves garlic (sliced)
- 4 5-oz. salmon fillets
- Chili oil, for serving

Directions:

1. Heat air fryer to 385°F. Toss onion with 1/2 tablespoon oil and a pinch each of salt and pepper and air-fry 5 minutes.
2. Toss with Swiss chard, garlic, 1 tablespoon oil, and 1/4 teaspoon each salt and pepper and air-fry until chard and onion are just tender, about 5 minutes more. Transfer to plates.
3. Season salmon with 1/2 teaspoon each salt and pepper and air-fry at 400°F until skin is crispy and salmon is opaque throughout, 8 to 10 minutes. Serve with chard and drizzle with chili oil if desired.

BEEF, PORK & LAMB RECIPES

Air Fryer Steak Fajitas

Ingredients:
- 1 lb. sliced beef (strips)
- 1 large or 2 small bell peppers
- 1/2 medium red onion
- 1/2 medium yellow onion
- Corn tortillas
- Cojita cheese (optional)
- 2 chopped serranos
- 1/4 tsp chili powder
- 1/4 tsp garlic powder
- 1/4 tsp oregano
- 1/2 ground cumin
- 2 tsp salt
- 1 tsp black pepper
- 2 tbsp. olive or vegetable oil

Directions:
1. In a large mixing bowl, combine spices and oil. Mix well.
2. Slice onions, peppers, and steak into strips and place in a bowl with seasoning. Coat the meat and veggies well.
3. Line air fryer with perforated parchment paper and then add the onions, peppers, and steak.
4. Air Fry for 5 minutes at 390 F. Remove basket and stir ingredients to ensure even cooking. Air Fry for an additional 4 minutes.
5. Serve with tortillas and top with Cotija cheese (optional)
6. Enjoy!

Air Fryer Crispy Chilli Beef

Servings: 2
Cooking Time: 15 Minutes

Ingredients:
- 250g thin-cut minute steak, thinly sliced into strips
- 2 tbsp cornflour
- 2 tbsp vegetable oil, plus a drizzle
- 2 garlic cloves, crushed
- thumb-sized piece of ginger, peeled and cut into matchsticks
- 1 red chilli, thinly sliced
- 1 red pepper, cut into chunks
- 4 spring onions, sliced, green and white parts separated
- 4 tbsp rice wine vinegar or white wine vinegar
- 1 tbsp soy sauce
- 2 tbsp sweet chilli sauce
- 2 tbsp tomato ketchup
- For the marinade
- ? tsp Chinese five-spice powder
- 2 tsp soy sauce
- 1 tsp sesame oil
- 1 tsp caster sugar

Directions:
1. First, combine the marinade ingredients in a bowl. Add the steak strips and toss to coat. Leave in the fridge for up to 24 hrs if you can, or carry on to step 2.
2. Sprinkle the cornflour over the steak and mix until each piece is coated in a floury paste. Pull the strips apart and arrange over a plate. Drizzle each piece of steak with a little oil. Heat the air fryer to 220C if it has a preheat setting.
3. Carefully put the beef on the cooking rack in the air fryer, cook for 6 mins, then turn and cook for another 4-6 mins until crispy.
4. Meanwhile, heat 2 tbsp vegetable oil in a wok over a high heat and stir-fry the garlic, ginger, chilli, pepper and white ends of the spring onions for 2-3 mins until the pepper softens. Be careful not to burn the ginger and garlic. Add the vinegar, soy, sweet chilli sauce and tomato ketchup, mix well and cook for another minute until bubbling.
5. Tip the beef into the wok and toss through the sauce. Continue cooking for another minute until piping hot, then serve scattered with the spring onion greens and a little extra sauce on the side.

Air Fryer Bacon

Servings: 2
Cooking Time: 10 Minutes

Ingredients:
- 3 strips of bacon any thickness

Directions:
1. First, preheat the air fryer to 350°F.
2. Next, slice each strip of bacon in half and lay them on your air fryer pan next to each other. They can be overlapping a little bit, but not all the way.
3. Air fry bacon at 350°F for: thin bacon: 6-7 minutes, medium bacon: 8 minutes, or thick bacon: 9-10 minutes. Flip bacon halfway through the bake time. If you like your bacon crispy, continue cooking for an extra 30 seconds to 1.5 minutes depending on the thickness of your bacon.

Tips & Notes
If you are planning to cook multiple rounds of bacon, make sure to discard excess grease that will build up on the bottom of your air fryer pan. This is to prevent smoking.
Make sure to keep an eye on your bacon as it can burn easily. The 350°F temperature should help prevent smoking, so don't cook your bacon any higher than that.

Air Fryer Beef Empanadas

Servings: 8
Cooking Time: 16 Minutes

Ingredients:
- 8 Goya empanada discs (in frozen section, thawed)
- 1 cup picadillo
- 1 egg white (whisked)
- 1 teaspoon water

Directions:
1. Spray the air fryer basket generously with olive oil spray to avoid sticking, or line the basket with air fryer parchment paper.
2. Place 2 tablespoons of the picadillo in the center of each disc. Fold in half and use a fork to seal the edges. Repeat with the remaining dough.
3. Whisk the egg whites with water, then brush the tops of the empanadas.
4. Air fry in a single layer, in batches as needed 350F 8 minutes, turning halfway or until golden. Remove from heat and repeat with the remaining empanadas.
5. Notes
6. How to Bake Empanadas in the Oven: If you don't have an air fryer, you can also bake them in the oven at 400 degrees on a nonstick baking sheet for about 18 to 20 minutes until golden.
7. How to Freeze Empanadas: You can flash freeze the uncooked empanadas on a sheet pan. Once frozen, transfer to a freezer-safe container for up to 3 months.
8. Air Fry From Frozen: Pop the frozen empanadas right into your air fryer and air fry 350F for about 12 minutes, turning halfway until golden and hot.

Air Fryer Bacon Wrapped Corn On The Cob

Servings: 2-4
Cooking Time: 20 Minutes

Ingredients:
- 2-4 ears fresh corn , shucked and cleaned
- 2-8 slices bacon , depending on how much corn & if you do double bacon or not
- salt , to taste
- black pepper , to taste
- oil spray or olive oil

Directions:
1. If needed, cut ends of corn to fit into your air fryer basket/tray. Or for smaller air fryers, cut the corn in half.
2. Coat all sides of the corn with light oil spray (if you're using only 1 bacon strip/ear). If needed, make sure to spray the ends of the corn is where it can often get dry.
3. Wrap bacon around the corn. Skewer one toothpick to secure each end of bacon to corn. Skewer the toothpick side-ways into the corn and bacon so it does't stick up too much. Season with salt and pepper to taste.
4. For 2 corn - Air Fry at 380°F for 10 minutes. Flip the corn. Continue Air Frying for

another 3-8 minutes or until bacon is crisp and corn is tender.

5. For 4 corn - Air Fry at 380°F for 10 minutes. Flip the corn. Continue Air Frying for another 6-10 minutes or until bacon is crisp and corn is tender. (Cooking time will depend on size of corn, thickness of the bacon, how full air fryer basket is, & different models/sizes of air fryers).

6. If needed, flip once more and Air Fry for a couple more minutes or until the bacon is crispy on all sides.

7. Remove toothpicks before eating. Add butter if desired and enjoy!

Air Fryer Crispy Chilli Beef Recipe

Ingredients:
- For the crispy beef
- 450g Beef Strips
- 4 tbsp Cornflour
- 2 tsp Sesame Oil
- 1 tsp Chinese 5 Spice
- 1 tsp Chilli Powder
- ½ tsp Salt
- ½ tsp Black Pepper
- For the sauce
- 200ml Beef Stock
- 4 tbsp Rice Wine Vinegar
- 2 tbsp Sweet Chilli Sauce
- 2 tbsp Sesame Oil
- 1 tbsp Soy Sauce
- 1 tbsp Tomato Puree
- 1 tbsp Honey
- 1 tsp Ginger
- 2 Cloves Garlic, Crushed
- 2 Spring Onions, Chopped
- 1 Red Chilli, Chopped
- 1 Red Pepper, Sliced
- 1 Green Pepper, Sliced

Directions:
1. Add the cornflour, Chinese 5 spice, black pepper, salt, and chili powder to a bowl and stir together.

2. Add beef strips to the bowl and ensure they are fully coated in cornflour mixture.

3. Drizzle 1 tsp of sesame oil at the bottom of the air fryer and add the beef strips in a single layer. Top with another tsp of sesame oil.

4. Cook the beef strips in the air fryer for 10 minutes at 200°C until crispy.

5. Meanwhile, add together the soy sauce, tomato puree, sweet chili, honey, rice wine vinegar, beef stock, and 1 tbsp of sesame oil and stir thoroughly. Set aside.

6. Heat up 1 tbsp of sesame oil in a frying pan and add the crushed garlic and chopped red chilli and stir together.

7. Add the 2 chopped spring onions, sliced red pepper and sliced green pepper to the pan, then add your mixed together sauce and stir through all the vegetables and cook this on high heat until the sauce has thickened.

8. Finally, add the crispy beef and coat it in the sauce.

9. When everything is coated and cooked, serve with egg noodles or rice and top with fresh chilies, spring onions, and sesame seeds.

Air Fryer Armadillo Eggs

Servings: 6
Cooking Time: 15 Minutes

Ingredients:
- 1 pound pork sausage ground
- 1 pound bacon 12 slices
- 6 medium jalapenos
- 4 ounces cream cheese room temperature
- 1/2 cup shredded cheddar cheese
- 1 cup Honey BBQ Sauce

Directions:
1. Rinse the jalapeno peppers and pat dry, then slice in half. Remove stems, membrane, and seeds, then set aside.

2. In a medium bowl, combine the cheddar and cream cheese. Generously spoon the cream cheese mixture into one of the halves of the jalapeno and then place two halves together.

3. Divide the pork sausage into six even portions. Flatten a portion of the sausage and fold around a jalapeno, pinch meat to completely seal and cover jalapeno, while

shaping into an oval egg shape. Repeat until all jalapenos are covered with sausage.

4. Wrap each covered jalapeno with two slices of bacon, wrapping each piece of bacon with tight wrap, securing with toothpicks.
5. Place in the air fryer basket and air fry at 380 for 15-17 minutes until sausage reaches an internal temperature of 160 degrees F and bacon is crispy. Use a meat thermometer to confirm doneness.
6. Using a basting brush or spoon, brush egg with barbecue sauce before serving.

NOTES
VARIATIONS and TIPS:
You can use flavored bacon like smoky bacon or Hickory bacon.
For higher heat level, and spicy peppers, leave some of the membrane.
There are other types of cheese blend you can add for a creamy cheese mixture. Shredded Monterey jack, mozzarella cheese, pepper jack, or even Mexican blend cheese, will make this a perfect appetizer recipe.
Dip in hot sauce, or for more flavor, try a Korean BBQ sauce or Raspberry Chipotle Sauce.
For a larger crowd, double batch recipe!

Air Fryer Corn Ribs
Servings: 4
Cooking Time: 12 Minutes

Ingredients:
- 2 ears of corn fresh
- 1 Tablespoon butter unsalted
- 1/4 teaspoon garlic powder
- 1/4 teaspoon salt Kosher
- 1/2 teaspoon smoked paprika
- 1/2 teaspoon ground black pepper
- 1/2 teaspoon dried parsley
- fresh parsley for garnish

Directions:
1. Take each whole ear of corn, remove from the husk.
2. Rub cobs to remove the corn silks from in between the corn kernels and cut off the ends.
3. Place corn on the cobs in a microwave safe bowl covered with a damp paper towel and microwave for 2 minutes.

4. Let corn cobs cool for 5 minutes on a chopping board or until they are cool enough to touch.
5. Use a sharp knife and slice into the corn cobs: cut the corn in halves lengthwise, and then cut halves into quarters, to make 4 pieces per cob of corn.
6. In a small bowl, combine butter, garlic powder, salt, paprika, black pepper and dried parsley.
7. Brush the corn ribs with the seasoning mixture, coating entire corn rib well.
8. In a single layer place the seasoned corn ribs into the air fryer basket.
9. Air fry at 400 degrees F for 12 minutes, flipping halfway through the cooking process.
10. Top with fresh parsley before serving.

NOTES
Optional Favorite Dipping Sauce: Ranch dressing, sour cream and chives, Carolina style bbq sauce, chipotle mayo or Greek yogurt with red pepper flakes.
Optional Additional Toppings: Lime wedges, fresh cilantro, fresh coriander or minced garlic butter.
Cooking Tips: Use a pastry brush to apply butter mixture to pieces of corn ribs. Cutting the corn into ribs makes it easier to eat especially for the little ones. For crispier corn cook for an additional 1-2 minutes.
Optional Additional Seasonings: Chili powder, lime juice, taco seasoning, chili oil, Elote seasoning, onion powder, cayenne pepper, chipotle powder or smoked salt.

Air Fryer Cheese Stuffed Meatballs
Servings: 4
Cooking Time: 7 Minutes

Ingredients:
- 1 pound ground beef
- 1 cup Italian Seasoned Breadcrumbs
- 1/2 cup parmesan cheese grated or shredded
- 1 large egg
- 1 teaspoon garlic minced
- 1/2 teaspoon kosher salt
- 1/4 teaspoon ground black pepper

- 4 pieces string cheese cut into inch in pieces

Directions:
1. In a medium mixing bowl, combine beef, breadcrumbs, parmesan cheese, egg, garlic, salt, and pepper. Stir until meatball mixture is well combined.
2. Use a large spoon or cookie scoop to measure them so they are all the same size (about 2-3 tablespoons of meat).
3. Roll each scoopful into about 2-inch sized meatballs (about the size of a golf ball). Place them on a plate or baking sheet until they are all rolled.
4. Cut string cheese into small pieces, about 1 inch in length. Push a cheese cube into the center of each meatball, and then close them back up around the piece of cheese, by reshaping the meatball to seal in the cheese.
5. Spray the air fryer basket with cooking spray and place the meatballs in a single layer to the basket.
6. Air fry at 380 degrees F for 7-10 minutes, until the hamburger meat is done. To make sure it's done, use a meat thermometer to read the internal temperature, minimum temperature should be about 160 degrees F.

NOTES

Optional Favorite Sauce for Dipping: Because meatballs are so versatile, you can eat them with your favorite marinara sauce, pizza sauce, alfredo sauce, pesto sauce or ranch dressing.

Kitchen Tips: This recipe will make a couple of batches of meatballs. Line basket with parchment paper so meatballs won't stick to the basket and makes for an easier clean up.

Substitutions: If you don't have lean ground beef, you can also use ground turkey, ground lamb, ground chicken, ground pork or a lean ground beef. Mini mozzarella balls are also a great stuffer.

Air Fryer Steak
Servings: 4
Cooking Time: 12 Minutes

Ingredients:
- 4 8-oz Top sirloin steaks (at least 1 inch thick, preferably 1.5 inches; other high-quality steaks with similar thickness will also work)
- 2 tsp Sea salt
- 1/2 tsp Black pepper
- 1/2 recipe Compound butter (optional)

Directions:
1. Remove your steak from the fridge about 30 minutes before cooking to bring it to room temperature. (This will ensure even cooking.)
2. Make compound butter according to the instructions here. Refrigerate until ready to serve.
3. Preheat the air fryer to 400 degrees F (204 degrees C).
4. Pat the steaks dry with paper towels. Season the steaks liberally with sea salt and black pepper on both sides.
5. Arrange the steaks in the air fryer in a single layer, so the pieces are not touching or only minimally touching (cook in batches if needed; don't crowd the basket). Air fry until the steaks reach your desired doneness (use a probe thermometer for best results). For 1.5-inch thick steaks, that's about 10-12 minutes for rare, 11-13 minutes for medium rare, 12-14 minutes for medium, 13-15 minutes for medium well, or 14-16 minutes for well done. Use a meat thermometer to check for the right temperature – 120 degrees F (52 degrees C) for rare, 130 degrees F (54 degrees C) for medium rare, 140 degrees F (60 degrees C) for medium, 150 degrees F (66 degrees C) for medium well, or 160 degrees F (71 degrees C) for well done. The temperature will rise by another 5 degrees F while resting (see next step).
6. Remove the steaks from the air and transfer to a plate. Top each with 1 tablespoon (14g) of compound butter.

7. Let the steaks rest for 5 minutes before slicing against the grain.

Air Fryer Steak Fries
Servings: 4
Cooking Time: 12 Minutes

Ingredients:
- Frozen Air Fryer Steak Fries:
- 1 bag Frozen Steak Fries
- Homemade Air Fryer Steak Fries:
- 4 Russet Potatoes
- 1 tbsp olive oil
- 1 tsp salt

Directions:
1. Frozen Steak Fries
2. For frozen steak fries, arrange the fries in the basket, without stacking or overlapping.
3. Cook the fries at 400 degrees F for 12 minutes. Shake the basket halfway through cooking. Depending on the air fryer, the actual cooking time may vary.
4. Homemade Steak Fries
5. Peel, rinse, and cut 4 medium Russet Potatoes into straight strips.
6. In a large bowl, soak the potato strips in cold water, for about 30 minutes. Drain, and pat the fries dry.
7. Toss the fries in 1-2 tbsp of olive oil, and then season with salt, or other desired seasonings.
8. Cook at 400 degrees F for 20-25 minutes, shaking the basket halfway through cooking, until golden and crispy. Serve warm with your favorite toppings.

Air Fryer Bacon Wrapped Jalapeños
Servings: 6
Cooking Time: 12 Minutes

Ingredients:
- 6 Jalapeño peppers
- 8 ounces cream cheese
- 4 ounces shredded cheddar cheese
- 6 pieces bacon

Directions:
1. Preheat the Air Fryer to 370 degrees Fahrenheit. Prepare the air fryer basket if needed with nonstick cooking spray, olive oil, or parchment paper.
2. Slice the jalapeño peppers in half, lengthwise. Use a small spoon to scoop the seeds and insides of each jalapeño half and then rinse.
3. Stuff each of the peppers with cream cheese. Top the cream cheese with shredded cheddar cheese.
4. Wrap each half of the stuffed jalapeño peppers with slices of bacon.
5. Place the bacon-wrapped jalapeño peppers in a single layer in the prepared air fryer basket.
6. Air Fry the peppers at 370 degrees Fahrenheit for 10-12 minutes or until the cream cheese filling has melted and the bacon is crispy.
7. Serve immediately.

NOTES

Are there flavor substitutions for jalapeno poppers?

Yes! You can add flavors to the cream cheese mixture and change things up easily. Consider adding in flavors such as onion powder, garlic powder, taco seasoning, or diced green onions.

Can I make bacon wrapped jalapeño poppers the day before?

Of course! You can follow the first few steps of making the jalapeno poppers and then store them in an airtight container in the refrigerator. When you're ready to cook, remove them from the refrigerator and cook as instructed at 370 degrees Fahrenheit for 10-12 minutes.

NOTE: This recipe for air fryer bacon wrapped jalapeno poppers was made using the 5.8qt Cosori Air Fryer. If you're using a different type of air fryer, you may need to adjust the cooking time up or down a minute or two to ensure your poppers cook accordingly.

Air Fryer Candied Bacon

Servings: 4
Cooking Time: 10 Minutes

Ingredients:
- 1 pound bacon
- ¼ cup brown sugar

Directions:
1. Place bacon slices in a shallow dish with brown sugar. Toss bacon slices well so both sides are coated with brown sugar.
2. Place slices in the air fryer basket, working in batches so they don't overlap while air frying.
3. Air fry at 380 degrees F for 10-12 minutes until bacon is crispy. Remove slices and place on a cooling rack or on a plate to cool before eating.

NOTES

No matter if you call this millionaire bacon or billionaire bacon, everyone will agree that this pig candy is yummy! I like to use dark brown sugar for this recipe as it makes it a delicious treat.

Cooking the bacon in the air fryer is also a great way to keep the bacon grease separate from the bacon, as it will fall through the bottom of the air fryer basket.

But did you know that you can actually use that leftover bacon grease for other air fryer recipes and cooking recipes? I'll save it and store it in a jar and then use it for cooking at other times. (It's really good to use when you're popping popcorn!)

Air Fryer Bacon Wrapped Brussel Sprouts

Servings: 4
Cooking Time: 13 Minutes

Ingredients:
- 8 slices bacon regular and sliced in half
- 16 small Brussels sprouts
- ¼ cup brown sugar

Directions:
1. Wrap one slice of halved bacon around each brussels sprout, seal with a toothpick if necessary. Repeat until all sprouts have been wrapped.
2. In a large glass bowl, toss wrapped sprouts with brown sugar, until they are well coated.
3. Place in the air fryer basket, without stacking or overlapping.
4. Air Fry at 380 degrees F for 13-16 minutes, until bacon is crispy.

NOTES
Variations

Change up the flavor of bacon - You can use salty bacon, crispy bacon, thick cut bacon, or any piece of bacon or strip of bacon that you want. Maple bacon sounds like some pretty good strips of bacon to add to this easy recipe!

Add toppings - Let's be truthful here and say that toppings are always a crowd-pleaser. Drizzling some olive oil with salt and black pepper on top of this delicious appetizer adds taste in an easy way.

You can add soy sauce to these tender brussels sprouts after they are done cooking, or add some sweetness with a drizzle of maple syrup!

Air Fryer Flank Steak

Servings: 4
Cooking Time: 15 Minutes

Ingredients:
- 1 pound flank steak
- 1 teaspoon Kosher salt
- 1/2 teaspoon ground black pepper
- 1 teaspoon garlic powder
- 1 teaspoon paprika

Directions:
1. Place steak in a shallow cooking dish once removed from the refrigerator to reach room temperature, for about 20-30 minutes before cooking. This helps the meat cook more evenly and ensures a tender steak.
2. Next make the rub for flank steak in medium mixing bowl. Combine the salt, pepper, garlic powder, and paprika.
3. Use paper towels to pat the steak dry.
4. Cover the steaks with saran wrap or place them inside an unsealed storage bag.

5. Use a meat tenderizer and gently pound the steak to break down the connective tissues and make the meat tender.
6. Gently rub the seasoning mix on both sides of the steak.
7. Spray the basket with oil, this will help crisp up the top and bottom of the steak.
8. Place the steak in the prepared air fryer basket and cook at 350 degrees F for 8 minutes, flipping the steak halfway through the cooking process.
9. Check the internal temperature of the steak with a meat thermometer.
10. Once the steak has reached 130 degrees F, (which brings the steak to a medium doneness) remove it from the basket or add 2-3 minutes cook time for a more well-done steak.
11. Place the cooked steak on a cutting board, cover it with foil, and allow flank steak rest time for at least 5 minutes so juices can redistribute, and steak remains juicy.
12. Slice flank steak against the grain with a sharp knife for maximum tenderness.
13. Move juicy flank steak to platter and serve.

NOTES

Because it is important to eat properly cooked meat, the surest and safest way to determine doneness, is with a meat thermometer. According to the FDA, proper temperatures for steak doneness, are:

Rare-125 degrees F
Medium Rare-135 degrees F
Medium-145 degrees F
Medium Well-155 degrees F
Well Done-160 degrees F

Optional Favorite Dipping Sauces: Creamy basil sauce, red wine sauce, steak sauce, creamed horseradish, red wine vinegar with sour cream, peppercorn sauce or cheesy garlic sauce.

Optional Additional Toppings: Fresh parsley, sauteed green bell pepper, slices of heirloom tomato mixture, cotija cheese, fresh cilantro leaves or grilled chopped pineapple.

Air Fryer Boneless Pork Chops

Servings: 2 - 2

Ingredients:
- 2 8 oz boneless pork chops (1.25" thick)
- Kosher salt and freshly ground black pepper
- 2 tsp. pork rub (optional)

Directions:
1. Set air fryer to 400F and preheat 3 to 4 minutes. Pat pork chops dry, and season both sides with salt and pepper and/or a spice rub.
2. Place pork chops into heated air fryer and cook, 6 minutes.
3. Flip chops and cook until internal temperature on an instant read thermometer reads 135F-145F, 5-8 minutes. If it's not warm enough, continue cooking, checking every 2-3 minutes, until cooked through.
4. Cover chops with a tent of aluminum foil and let rest 5 minutes, to allow chops to reabsorb juices, before slicing and eating.

Air Fryer Ham Steaks

Servings: 1
Cooking Time: 10 Minutes

Ingredients:
- 1 ham steak
- 2 tablespoons butter, melted
- 2 tablespoons brown sugar, packed
- 1 teaspoon honey* (optional)

Directions:
1. Preheat your air fryer to 380 degrees.
2. Remove the ham steak from its packaging.
3. Mix the brown sugar and melted butter together in a bowl.
4. Place ham steak in the air fryer and baste half of the mixture on top of the ham slice.
5. Cook for 10-12 minutes, flipping and basting the ham steak again halfway through.
6. Remove from the air fryer and drizzle optional honey on top.

NOTES
*add honey only if not using a honey ham

Air Fryer Chuck Roast

Servings: 6
Cooking Time: 45 Minutes

Ingredients:
- 2 pounds beef chuck roast
- 1 tablespoon olive oil
- ½ tablespoon Worcestershire sauce
- 1 ½ teaspoons kosher salt
- 1 ½ teaspoons garlic powder
- 1 teaspoon onion powder
- 1 teaspoon dried thyme
- 1 teaspoon dried rosemary
- 1 teaspoon black pepper

Directions:
1. Line the inside of your air fryer with aluminum foil. Preheat the air fryer to 390 degrees F.
2. In a small bowl, whisk together olive oil and Worcestershire sauce. In a second small bowl, combine the salt, garlic powder, onion powder, thyme, rosemary, and pepper.
3. Rub the roast with the olive oil-Worcestershire sauce mixture, then rub the herb mixture over the entire roast. Place the roast in the basket of your air fryer.
4. Air fry for 15 minutes, then carefully flip the roast. Air fry at 320 degrees F for another 45-60 minutes, depending on the size of the roast.
5. Remove, allow to rest for 10 minutes, then slice and serve with your favorite sides.

Air Fryer Herb Crusted Roast Beef

Servings: 6
Cooking Time: 1 Hour 20 Minutes

Ingredients:
- 1.2 kg piece beef scotch fillet
- 1 tablespoon olive oil
- 2/3 cup (80g) panko breadcrumbs
- ¼ cup (20g) finely grated parmesan
- 2 tablespoon chopped flat-leaf parsley
- 1 tablespoon chopped tarragon
- ¼ cup chopped chives
- 2 cloves garlic, crushed
- ¼ cup (70g) wholegrain mustard
- 1 teaspoon smoked paprika
- olive oil cooking spray
- 150 grams swiss brown mushrooms, halved (or quartered if large)
- 150 grams button mushrooms, halved (or quartered if large)
- ¾ cup (180ml) thickened cream
- to serve: roast potatoes

Directions:
1. Preheat a 7-litre air fryer to 200°C/400°F for 5 minutes.
2. Brush beef with 2 teaspoons of the the oil and season.
3. Taking care, place beef in the air fryer basket; at 200°C/400°F, cook for 15 minutes, turning halfway through cooking time, until browned all over.
4. Meanwhile, combine the breadcrumbs, parmesan, parsley, tarragon, half the chives and half the garlic in a bowl, then season. Transfer beef to a plate and pat dry with paper towel. Working quickly, spread 2 tablespoons of the mustard over the top and sides of the beef, sprinkle with paprika, then firmly press on breadcrumb mixture. Spray breadcrumbs generously with cooking spray.
5. Return beef to the air fryer basket, then cover basket tightly with foil. Reset the temperature to 180°C/350°F; cook for 30 minutes. Remove foil.
6. Toss mushrooms in remaining oil and add to the air fryer basket with beef; cook, without foil, for a further 10 minutes until beef is medium or cooked to your liking (see testing meat when ready to right) and mushrooms are browned. Transfer beef to a dish; cover loosely with foil and rest for 15 minutes.
7. Meanwhile, to make creamy mushrooms, combine cream and remaining garlic and mustard in a medium saucepan over medium heat; add the mushrooms and any
8. cooking juices from the bottom of the air fryer pan and bring to the boil. Reduce heat; simmer, stirring occasionally, for 5 minutes or until sauce thickens slightly.
9. Stir in remaining chives and season to taste.

10. Thinly slice beef and serve with creamy mushrooms and roast potatoes.testing meat when readyInsert a meat thermometer into the thickest part of the beef. The internal temperature should reach:
11. rare 55–60°C/130–140°F
12. medium–rare 60–65°C/140–150°F
13. medium 65–70°C/150–160°F
14. medium–well done 70–75°C/160–170°F
15. well done 75°C/170°F

Air Fryer Gingery Pork Meatballs

Servings: 4

Ingredients:
- FOR NOODLES
- 6 oz. rice noodles
- 1/2 c. Asian-style sesame dressing
- 1 large carrot, shaved with julienne peeler or cut into matchsticks
- 1/2 English cucumber, shaved with julienne peeler or cut into matchsticks
- 1 scallion, thinly sliced
- 1/4 c. cilantro, chopped
- FOR MEATBALLS
- 1 large egg
- 2 tsp. grated lime zest plus 2 Tbsp lime juice
- 1 1/2 tbsp. honey
- 1 tsp. fish sauce
- Kosher salt
- 1/2 c. panko
- 1 cloves garlic, grated
- 2 scallions, finely chopped
- 1 tbsp. grated fresh ginger
- 1 small jalape?o, seeds removed, finely chopped
- 1 lb. ground pork
- 1/4 c. cilantro, chopped

Directions:
1. Prepare noodles: Cook noodles per package directions. Rinse under cold water to cool, drain well and transfer to large bowl. Toss with dressing, carrot, cucumber and scallion; set aside.
2. Prepare meatballs: In large bowl, whisk together egg, lime zest and lime juice, honey, fish sauce and ? teaspoon salt; stir

in panko and let sit 1 minute. Stir in garlic, scallions, ginger and jalape?o, then add pork and cilantro and mix to combine.
3. Shape into Tbsp-size balls and air-fry at 400F (in batches, if necessary; balls can touch but should not be stacked), shaking basket occasionally, until browned and cooked through, 8 to 12 minutes. Fold cilantro into noodles and serve with meatballs.

Air Fryer Taco Casserole

Servings: 4
Cooking Time: 20 Minutes

Ingredients:
- 1 lb lean ground beef 95% lean
- 3 tbsp taco seasoning
- 1/4 cup water
- 1/2 cup bell pepper chopped
- 10 oz diced tomatoes and green chilis not drained
- 4 large eggs
- 1/4 cup sour cream
- 1/3 cup heavy cream
- 1/2 cup cheddar cheese shredded
- 1 tbsp green onions optional

Directions:
1. Brown the lean ground beef in a skillet over medium heat, about 5 minutes or until no longer pink. Drain.
2. Add the water, taco seasoning, diced bell pepper, and canned tomatoes with green chilis. Stir and simmer for 3 minutes.
3. Preheat the Air Fryer to 300 degrees Fahrenheit. Prepare the air fryer casserole/cake dish.
4. In a medium mixing bowl, whisk the eggs, sour cream, and heavy cream together. Set aside.
5. Pour the taco meat mixture into the bottom of the prepared casserole pan. Top the meat mixture with the egg mixture.
6. Place the casserole into the air fryer basket and cook for 18 minutes. Top with cheese and cook an additional 2 minutes, or until the cheese is fully melted.
7. Top with green onions and serve.

NOTES
Store in an airtight container in the refrigerator for up to 3 days.
Consider adding additional flavors like diced jalapenos for extra spice.
Mix up the flavors by adding a little mozzarella and cream cheese to the dish.

Air Fryer Pork Chops In 9 Minutes

Servings: 4
Cooking Time: 9 Minutes

Ingredients:
- 4 medium pork chops boneless
- 1 tablespoon olive oil
- 2 teaspoons smoked paprika
- 2 teapoons cumin
- 1 teaspoon onion powder
- 1/2 teaspoon salt
- 1/2 teaspoon pepper

Directions:
1. Preheat the air fryer to 190C/375F.
2. Pat dry the boneless pork chops, then add into a bowl and rub the oil generously over them all.
3. Mix the spices in a bowl, then rub on both sides of the pork.
4. Place the pork chops in the air fryer basket and cook for 9 minutes, flipping halfway through.
5. Remove the pork from the air fryer and serve immediately.
6. Notes
7. TO STORE: Use air-tight containers to refrigerate the pork chops. They will keep well for up to five days.
8. TO FREEZE: Place leftovers in a ziplock bag and store them in the freezer for up to two months.
9. TO REHEAT: Either microwave the chops for 20-30 seconds or reheat in a non-stick pan until hot.

Air Fryer Bacon Wrapped Serranos

Ingredients:
- 12 Serrano peppers
- 12 Slices partially Cooked bacon
- 2 String Mozarella Cheeses

Directions:
1. Partially cook the bacon in the air fryer at 300° for 3 minutes on each side. Place onto paper towel and set aside.
2. Cut the tops off the serrano peppers and carefully slice down one side of the pepper(do not cut all the way through). Fold open the pepper and remove seeds.
3. Peel pieces of the string cheese and stuff the peppers. Wrap the bacon around each pepper tightly then place into air fryer basket.
4. Air fry at 350° for 5 minutes or until desired bacon crispiness.

Air Fryer Bacon Cauliflower Mac And Cheese

Servings: 6
Cooking Time: 10 Minutes

Ingredients:
- 4 strips bacon
- 1 cup water
- 1 small cauliflower diced
- 4 ounces cream cheese
- ¼ cup   heavy cream
- 2 cups   cheddar cheese shredded
- 1 teaspoon salt
- ¼ teaspoon   cayenne pepper
- 1 teaspoon   paprika
- green onions or parsley finely chopped, for garnish

Directions:
1. Cook the bacon in the air fryer for 5 minutes. Dice into small pieces.
2. In a microwave-safe bowl - add one cup of water and the cauliflower. Microwave for five minutes. Check for tenderness. If still hard cook another few minutes. Drain.
3. Preheat Air Fryer to 400°F.
4. In the same bowl, combine the cream cheese, heavy cream, one cup of cheese, salt,

cayenne, bacon, and paprika. Microwave one more minute.

5. Put the cauliflower mixture in a Vortex-safe dish. Place on the lowest shelf - use a quick cover if you have one to keep the top from browning too quick.

6. Cook for 4 minutes. Remove top and cook for 2 more until golden brown.

Notes

This can also be done in an Instant Pot - close lid and set for 2 minutes. Quick release. Add all of the ingredients and close the lid and manual cook for one more minute. Quick-release. Enjoy!

Air Fryer Prosciutto Wrapped Asparagus

Servings: 4
Cooking Time: 8 Minutes

Ingredients:
- 1 pound asparagus
- 6 ounces prosciutto

Directions:
1. Preheat air fryer to 400°F.
2. Wash and trim the end of the asparagus.
3. Wrap one slice of prosciutto around one asparagus and place in the air fryer basket.
4. Cook for 7-8 minutes or until asparagus is tender and prosciutto is crispy.

Air Fryer Short Ribs

Servings: 2-4
Cooking Time: 15 Minutes

Ingredients:
- 1 pound short ribs (pork or beef), 1.5-inch pieces
- 1 tablespoon vegetable oil
- 1 tablespoon soy sauce (or oyster sauce)
- 1 tablespoon Shaoxing wine (optional)
- 1/2 teaspoon salt
- 1/2 teaspoon ground black pepper
- 1/2 teaspoon garlic powder
- 1/2 teaspoon paprika
- 1/4 teaspoon ground cumin powder
- 1/4 teaspoon crushed red pepper (optional)
- 1 teaspoon cornstarch

Directions:

1. In a large mixing bowl or Ziploc bag, combine the ribs with all the ingredients and mix well to coat evenly. If you use the Ziploc bag, press the seasoning around to coat evenly. Let the marinated ribs rest for at least 15 minutes to soak in all the flavour.

2. Place the marinated ribs in a single layer in the air fryer basket. Cook at 350F for 13-15 minutes until golden brown and crispy. Shake the basket halfway to cook the ribs evenly. (See recipe tips for oven bake and deep fry instructions).

3. Serve immediately with your favorite dipping sauce, such as spicy mayo, sweet chili sauce, ketchup, or ranch.

NOTES

How to bake in the oven: Place the marinated short ribs in a single layer on a parchment-lined quarter sheet baking pan and bake at 400F for 15-20 minutes until crispy and golden brown.

How to deep fry: Heat oil in a medium cooking pot (at least 2-inches deep) over medium high heat for 3-4 minutes until the oil shimmers. Deep fry the marinated ribs until golden brown, about 5-7 minutes. Turn the ribs occasionally to get an even golden crust on all sides. Transfer the ribs on a paper towel lined plate to drain excess oil.

How to store: Keep air fryer short ribs in an airtight container in the fridge for up to 3-4 days.

How to reheat: Reheat these dry short ribs in the air fryer at 350F for 5 to 10 minutes until warm and crispy. You can also reheat them in a 350F preheated oven for 10 to 15 minutes.

Air Fryer Bacon Wrapped Brussels Sprouts

Servings: 8
Cooking Time: 7 Minutes

Ingredients:
- 1 pound brussels sprouts
- ½ pound bacon
- ⅓ cup maple syrup

Directions:
1. Preheat the air fryer to 375°F.
2. Wash and trim brussels cutting them in half.

3. Cut each piece of bacon into thirds. Wrap bacon around the brussels sprouts.
4. Place seam side down in the air fryer basket and brush with maple syrup.
5. Bake 7-10 minutes or until bacon is crisp and brussels sprouts are tender.

Notes

Brussels sprouts should be cooked in a single layer. If needed, cook in batches.

Air Fryer Steak Bites

Servings: 4
Cooking Time: 6 Minutes

Ingredients:
- 1 pound sirloin steak or strip loin or ribeye
- 1 tablespoon vegetable oil
- 1 tablespoon soy sauce
- 1 ½ teaspoons Worcestershire sauce
- 2 cloves garlic minced
- 1 tablespoon melted salted butter
- salt & pepper to taste
- 1 tablespoon fresh parsley

Directions:
1. Cut steak into 1-inch cubes. Toss with oil, soy sauce, Worcestershire sauce, garlic, salt & pepper. Marinate 15 minutes.
2. Preheat air fryer to 400°F.
3. Remove the steak bites from the marinade and dab dry. Toss with melted butter.
4. Add steak bites to the air fryer basket in a single layer and cook 6-7 minutes or until browned. Do not overcook.
5. Toss with parsley and additional butter if desired. Serve with horseradish sauce below.

Notes

Cook steak bites in batches if needed. Do not overcrowd the air fryer.

Whisk together the following for Horseradish Dipping Sauce:

¼ cup sour cream
2 tablespoons mayonnaise
1 ½ tablespoons prepared horseradish
1 teaspoon fresh lemon juice
1 small clove garlic
salt & pepper to taste

Air Fryer Country Style Ribs

Servings: 5
Cooking Time: 20 Minutes

Ingredients:
- 2 lbs ribs country-style
- 1 tsp smoked paprika
- 1 1/2 tsp garlic powder
- 2 tsp ground black pepper
- 5 oz barbecue sauce

Directions:
1. Rinse the ribs and then pat them dry. Add the garlic powder, smoked paprika, and ground black seasoning to a small bowl and set aside.
2. Preheat the air fryer to 380 degrees Fahrenheit. Prepare the basket of the air fryer with nonstick cooking spray.
3. Rub the ribs with a small amount of the seasoning mixture.
4. Place the ribs in a single layer in the basket of the air fryer. Cook at 380 degrees for 20 minutes. Remove the basket and brush barbecue sauce onto the tops and sides of the ribs. Place back into the air fryer and cook for an additional 2 minutes. Check the internal temperature with a meat thermometer to ensure the pork has reached 145 degrees Fahrenheit.
5. Serve with your favorite sides.

NOTES

Store leftover country-style ribs in an airtight container in the refrigerator for up to 3 days.

This recipe was made using a Cosori 1700 watt 5.8 qt basket style air fryer. All air fryers can cook differently. It's always best to test a small batch before cooking the entire meal to decide if our air fryer requires more or less time.

Air Fryer Frozen Meatballs

Servings: 3
Cooking Time: 10 Minutes

Ingredients:

- 1 lb. (454 g) Frozen Meatballs (16 oz./454g)
- oil spray , to coat the meatballs
- BBQ or Tomato Sauce , optional
- Oil Sprayer

Directions:

1. Place the frozen meatballs in the air fryer basket and spread out into a single even layer (cook in batches if needed). Coat the meatballs evenly with oil spray.
2. Air Fry at 380°F/195°C for 8-12 minutes (depending on size) or until heated all the way through, gently shaking and turning the meatballs halfway through cooking.
3. If desired, heat your favorite sauce (BBQ, tomato, etc.) & toss or brush the sauce with the meatballs before serving.

NOTES

Cook Frozen - Do not thaw first.

Shake or turn as needed. Don't overcrowd the air fryer basket.

Recipe timing is based on a non-preheated air fryer. If cooking in multiple batches back to back, the following batches may cook a little quicker.

Adjust cooking time based off your specific air fryer.

Remember to set a timer to shake/flip/toss as directed in recipe.

SANDWICHES & BURGERS RECIPES

Keto Friendly Game Day Burgers

Ingredients:
- Mini Beef Burgers:
- 1.5 pounds ground beef
- 1/4 cup onion, diced
- 1 tsp salt
- 1/4 tsp pepper
- 1 tsp brown Mustard
- Low Carb Sauce:
- 1/2 cup mayonnaise
- 1 tsp white wine vinegar
- 1 tsp paprika
- 1 tsp garlic powder
- 1 tsp onion powder
- 4 tbsp dill pickle relish

Directions:
1. Using your hands mix together the beef, onion, salt, pepper, and brown sugar (optional.)
2. Form into 15-20 mini balls.
3. Cook in your air fryer, flipping half way to your desired doneness, 7-8 minutes at 390 degrees.
4. While the burgers are cooking, mix your mayonnaise, white vinegar, paprika, garlic powder, onion powder, and dill pickle relish together. Set to the side.
5. Place each burger on a skewer with cheese, lettuce, pickles, and the special sauce.
6. Enjoy!

Air Fryer Hamburgers

Servings: 4
Cooking Time: 8 Minutes

Ingredients:
- 1-pound ground beef, thawed (preferably 80/20)
- 1 clove garlic, minced
- 1/2 teaspoon salt
- 1/4 teaspoon pepper

Directions:
1. Preheat air fryer to 360 degrees.
2. Mix together the ground beef, minced garlic, salt, and pepper with your hands.

3. Form ground beef into 4 patties and press them down with the back of a pie plate to make them evenly flat.
4. Place hamburgers in a single layer inside the air fryer.
5. Cook for 8-12 minutes, flipping halfway through cooking for medium-well hamburgers.*
6. Carefully remove hamburgers from the air fryer,** place onto hamburger buns (if using), and add desired toppings.

NOTES
*thicker hamburgers may take longer to cook if not pressed down properly
** if making cheeseburgers, place a piece of cheese on each burger in the air fryer, turn the air fryer off, and let the burgers sit in the air fryer for 1 to 2 minutes until melted

Air Fried Crispy Chicken Sandwiches

Servings: 4

Ingredients:
- 2 large chicken breasts, cut in half and pounded to an even thickness
- 1 cup buttermilk
- 1 tablespoon kosher salt or 1 teaspoon table salt
- ¾ cup panko breadcrumbs
- ½ cup all-purpose flour
- ½ teaspoon salt
- ¼ teaspoon dried oregano
- ½ teaspoon paprika
- ¼ teaspoon garlic powder
- ¼ teaspoon dried thyme
- ¼ teaspoon ground ginger
- ½ teaspoon ground black pepper
- Oil spray
- 4 brioche burger buns
- Assorted toppings such as lettuce, tomato, onions and additional condiments

Directions:
1. Place the chicken breasts in a zipper top bag and pour in buttermilk and salt. Squeeze

the air out and seal the bag. Marinate in the refrigerator for at least an hour or preferably overnight.

2. In a shallow bowl combine the panko breadcrumbs, flour and spices.
3. Remove the chicken breasts from the buttermilk. Remove excess buttermilk and dredge in the breadcrumb mixture.
4. Arrange the chicken breasts in one layer on a parchment-lined baking sheet, thoroughly coating chicken with oil spray on both sides.
5. Air Fry at 375°F for 20 – 25 minutes or until internal temperature reads 165°F and the chicken breasts are golden brown and crispy. For more even cooking, flip the chicken halfway through and spray with more oil if desired.
6. Serve chicken sandwiches on toasted brioche buns with lettuce, tomatoes, red onion and other favorite condiments.

Air Fryer Grilled Cheese Sandwich

Servings: 2
Cooking Time: 7 Minutes

Ingredients:
- 8 slices white bread
- 1 tablespoon butter
- 4 slices cheese

Directions:
1. Spread a light layer of the butter on one side of each piece of bread.
2. Place the buttered side down in the air fryer basket.
3. Cover the slice of bread with a piece of cheese. Then top the cheese with another slice of bread, with the buttered side up.
4. Air Fry at 370 degrees F for 3-5 minutes. Then flip, and air fry for 2-3 additional minutes, until bread reaches desired crispness.

NOTES
Make this a heartier meal by adding a few slices of bacon to the sandwich, avocado slices, or on inside of slices, spread bread with pesto sauce before adding cheese.

Depending on the type of bread you use, you may want to adjust the cook times. For softer bread, or French Bread, air fry until it reaches your desired crispness.

Air Fryer Bacon, Egg And Cheese Biscuit Breakfast Sandwiches

Servings: 8

Ingredients:
- 1 can (16.3 oz) refrigerated Pillsbury™ Grands!™ Southern Homestyle Original Biscuits (8 Count)
- 6 eggs
- 1/4 teaspoon salt
- 1/8 teaspoon pepper, if desired
- 1 tablespoon butter
- 8 slices cooked bacon, cut in half crosswise
- 8 slices (3/4 oz each) American cheese

Directions:
1. Spray bottom of air fryer basket with cooking spray. Separate dough into 8 biscuits. Place 4 biscuits in air fryer basket, spacing apart.
2. Set air fryer to 330°F; cook 6 minutes. Using tongs or spatula, turn over each biscuit. Cook 4 to 5 minutes or until biscuits are deep golden brown and cooked through. Remove from air fryer; cover loosely with foil to keep warm while cooking second batch. Cook remaining biscuits as directed above.
3. Meanwhile, in medium bowl, beat eggs, salt and pepper thoroughly with fork or whisk until well mixed. In 10-inch skillet, heat butter over medium heat just until butter begins to sizzle. Pour egg mixture into skillet. Cook until set, stirring occasionally.
4. To serve, split warm biscuits; top bottom half of each with scrambled eggs, bacon and cheese. Cover with top halves of biscuits.

Air Fryer Frozen Burger

Servings: 2
Cooking Time: 15 Minutes

Ingredients:
- 2 frozen burger patties

Directions:
1. Place frozen burgers in a single layer in the basket of the air fryer.
2. Air fry the burgers at 350 degrees Fahrenheit for 15 minutes, flipping the burgers halfway through cook time.
3. If desired, add sliced cheese during the last minute of cooking time.
4. Carefully remove the burgers from the air fryer and serve them with your favorite toppings.

NOTES
If adding cheese, top with sliced cheese during the last minute of cook time.
Serve bunless for a healthier burger.

Air Fryer Chicken Burgers

Servings: 4
Cooking Time: 10 Minutes

Ingredients:
- 1 pound ground chicken
- 1 large egg
- 1 cup mozzarella cheese shredded
- 1/2 cup onion finely chopped
- 1/2 cup panko breadcrumbs
- 1 teaspoon minced garlic
- 1/2 teaspoon kosher salt
- 1/4 teaspoon ground black pepper

Directions:
1. Preheat air fryer to 365 degrees F.
2. In a large bowl, combine the chicken, egg, cheese, onion, panko crumbs, garlic, salt and pepper. Mix chicken mixture together with your hands until fully combined.
3. Divide the chicken mixture into 4 equal parts and shape them into 5-inch diameter burgers.
4. Spray the air fryer basket with non-stick cooking spray and place the chicken patties in air fryer in a single layer.
5. Air fry the chicken burgers at 365 degrees F for 8-10 minutes or until cooked through, depending on the thickness of the patties.
6. Use a meat thermometer to confirm internal temperature of burger patties which should be a safe temperature of 165 degrees F.
7. Allow chicken burgers to cool for a couple of minutes then carefully remove them from the basket.
8. Serve while hot or let them continue to rest on a baking rack.

NOTES
Optional Additional Favorite Sauces: BBQ sauce, mustard yogurt sauce, chili sauce, ketchup, spicy sriracha sauce (based on your spice level), honey mustard, marinara sauce, relish or a sweet and spicy pickle.
Optional Favorite Toppings: Shredded lettuce, slice of tomato, raw or caramelized onions, sundried tomato strips, bacon, avocado, pepper jack cheese, American cheese or shredded cheese.
Cooking Tips: Use a silicone mat to make it an easy clean up and prevent food sticking to your basket. For crispy chicken patties brush a little olive oil on the patties prior to placing them in your air fryer.
I make this recipe in my Cosori 5.8 qt. air fryer. Depending on your air fryer, size and wattages, your cooking time may need to be adjusted 1-2 minutes.

Greek Lamb Burgers With Baked Eggplant Fries

Servings: 4

Ingredients:
- Nonstick cooking spray
- 1 pound ground lamb
- 2 ounces feta cheese, crumbled (about ½ cup)
- ½ cup grated red onion (from 1 small onion), divided
- 1 ½ tablespoon olive oil, divided
- 2 ½ teaspoons kosher salt, divided
- ¾ teaspoon freshly ground black pepper, divided
- 1 ½ cups panko

- 2 large egg whites
- 1 medium eggplant, cut into ½-by-1-by-2-in. wedges
- ½ cup grated English cucumber (from ½ cucumber)
- 1 cup plain whole-milk Greek yogurt
- 2 teaspoons fresh lemon juice (from 1 lemon)
- Hamburger buns and lettuce, for serving

Directions:

1. Preheat oven to 425°F. Lightly coat a rimmed baking sheet with cooking spray. Stir together lamb, cheese, ¼ cup onion, 1 tablespoon oil, 1 teaspoon salt, and ½ teaspoon pepper in a bowl until just combined; shape into 4 patties.
2. Combine panko and remaining 1½ teaspoons salt in a large ziplock plastic bag. Whisk egg whites in a large bowl until foamy. Dip eggplant wedges, 1 at a time, in egg whites and transfer to bag with panko. Once all eggplant has been added to bag, seal and shake well to coat. Arrange eggplant in an even layer on prepared baking sheet and coat generously with cooking spray. Bake until golden brown, about 20 minutes, flipping halfway through.
3. Meanwhile, heat remaining ½ tablespoon oil in a large nonstick skillet over medium-high. Add lamb patties and cook, flipping once, until browned, about 4 minutes per side for medium.
4. Place cucumber and remaining ¼ cup onion on a paper towel. Squeeze gently to release liquid. Transfer to a small bowl and stir in yogurt, lemon juice, and remaining ¼ teaspoon pepper.
5. Place patties on buns with lettuce and yogurt sauce. Serve with eggplant fries and remaining yogurt sauce.

Air Fryer Biscuit Egg Sandwiches
Servings: 4

Ingredients:
- Deselect All
- Nonstick cooking spray, for the molds
- 4 large eggs
- Kosher salt
- 4 thin slices deli ham
- One 16.3-ounce tube refrigerated flaky biscuit dough, such as Pillsbury
- Hot sauce, for serving

Directions:

1. Special equipment: 4 silicone baking cups, 6-quart air fryer
2. Spray 4 silicone baking cups with nonstick spray. Transfer the cups to the basket of a 6-quart air fryer.
3. Whisk together the eggs in a large glass measuring cup until no white streaks remain. Season with 1/2 teaspoon salt. Divide the eggs among the baking cups. Insert a piece of ham into each cup, crumpling it to make it fit (some of the ham should stick out above the surface of the eggs).
4. Tear off 4 biscuits from the tube of dough. Place each biscuit in the basket of the air fryer in a single layer. Set the air fryer to 300 degrees F and cook for 10 minutes. The biscuits should be golden brown; transfer to a cutting board.
5. Gently lift each egg muffin from its mold so you can see if it's set. If there's no liquid egg on the bottom, transfer the mold to the cutting board. If there is liquid egg on the bottom, cook for up to 1 minute more.
6. Slice each biscuit in half crosswise. Remove the egg muffins from the molds and slice in half crosswise. Arrange the two egg halves on each bottom biscuit, drizzle with plenty of hot sauce and sandwich with the top biscuit.

SALADS & SIDE DISHES RECIPES

Cardamom Roasted Beetroot Salad With Harissa Tahini Sauce

Servings: 4

Ingredients:

- For the roasted beets
- 500g beetroot (peeled, chopped into 2cm pieces)
- 1 x 400g organic chickpeas (drained, rinsed, patted dry)
- 1 1/2 tbsp olive oil
- 1 tbsp agave nectar
- 2 tsp ground cumin
- 16 Seeds from green cardamom pods (ground in pestle and mortar)
- 1 1/4 tsp sea salt
- 1/2 tsp garlic powder
- 1/4 tsp ground black pepper
- 1 Zest of lemon
- For the sauce
- 80g light tahini
- 190ml lukewarm water
- 1 tbsp rose harissa
- 2 tsp agave nectar
- 1 clove garlic (peeled)
- 1 tsp red wine vinegar
- 1/4 tsp ground cumin
- 1/4 - 1/2 tsp sea salt
- 1/2 - 1 Juice of whole lemon
- For the salad
- 100g pomegranate seeds (roughly 1/2 pomegranate)
- 60g rocket
- 30g walnuts (roughly chopped)
- 20g fresh parsley (roughly chopped)
- 1/2 tsp za'atar
- COOKING MODE
- When entering cooking mode - We will enable your screen to stay 'always on' to avoid any unnecessary interruptions whilst you cook!

Directions:

1. Toss together all of the ingredients for the roasted beets in a large bowl until everything is fully coated.

2. Place the crisper tray into the zone 1 drawer then add the vegetables and insert the drawer back into the unit. Select ROAST, set the temperature to 180°C and the temperature to 25 minutes. Select START/STOP to begin cooking. Shake the drawer every 10 minutes until the cooking time is complete. Remove the drawer and set to one side.

3. Place the ingredients for the sauce into a bullet style blender and blend until smooth. Start with the juice of half a lemon and add more if you feel it needs it. Again if you'd prefer a thinner sauce blend in more water.

4. Toss together the roasted beetroot mixture in a large salad bowl with the remaining salad ingredients then serve immediately with plenty of the sauce drizzled over.

Air Fryer Roasted Butternut Squash Salad

Servings: 4
Cooking Time: 15 Minutes

Ingredients:

- 1 small butternut squash, peeled, seeded, cut into 1-inch pieces
- 4 tablespoons olive oil
- 1 teaspoon 's House Seasoning
- 1/4 teaspoon cayenne pepper
- 2 tablespoons fresh lemon juice
- 1 small shallot, minced
- 1/4 teaspoon salt
- 6 ounces arugula
- 1 small Granny Smith apple, cored and thinly sliced
- 1/2 cup toasted sliced almonds
- 1/2 cup grated Parmesan cheese

Directions:

1. In a large bowl, combine squash, 2 tablespoons of the olive oil, House Seasoning, and cayenne pepper; toss to coat well.

2. Place squash in air fryer basket, set air fryer temperature to 400 degrees, and cook for 15 minutes, shaking occasionally. Let cool.
3. In a large bowl, whisk together lemon juice, shallot, salt, and remaining olive oil. Add arugula and toss to coat. Divide arugula between 4 salad plates and top with squash and apple slices. Sprinkle with sliced almonds and Parmesan cheese. Serve chilled.

Air Fryer Pigs In A Blanket
Servings: 10
Cooking Time: 8 Minutes

Ingredients:
- 1 can crescent rolls
- 24 cocktail sausages

Directions:
1. Preheat the air fryer to 350 degrees Fahrenheit. Prepare the air fryer basket with nonstick cooking spray, or once the air fryer has been preheated, add parchment paper.
2. Take a pizza cutter and slice each crescent dough sheet into thirds.
3. Take the cut crescent dough and wrap the dough around the sausage.
4. Place the crescent dogs into the prepared air fryer basket in a single layer and make sure to allow an inch or two between each crescent sausage. You may need to cook in batches if needed.
5. Air fry on 350 degrees Fahrenheit for 3-4 minutes, flip, and then air fry for an additional 3-4 minutes, or until the crescents are golden brown.
6. Carefully remove from the air fryer basket and serve with your favorite dipping sauces.

NOTES
This recipe was made using the Cosori 5.8 qt air fryer. If you are using a different air fryer, your cook time may need to be adjusted up or down depending on the wattage and power of the heating element.
WHAT DIPPING SAUCES CAN I USE FOR PIGS IN A BLANKET?

I love to use ketchup and mustard, but you can also use bbq sauce, cheese sauce, honey mustard sauce, ranch dressing, and more.
CAN I COOK FROZEN PIGS IN A BLANKET IN THE AIR FRYER?
Absolutely! If you are cooking these pigs in a blanket from frozen, you will want to add a minute or two to the cooking time to ensure they are cooked completely.

Air Fryer Asparagus Salad With Feta Vinaigrette
Servings: 4

Ingredients:
- 1 lb. asparagus
- 2 tbsp. olive oil, divided
- Kosher salt and pepper
- 1 tbsp. rice vinegar
- 1 small shallot, finely chopped
- 1/4 c. fresh mint, finely chopped
- 2 oz. feta, crumbled
- 2 tbsp. fresh dill, roughly chopped

Directions:
1. Heat oven to 425°F. On a small rimmed baking sheet, toss asparagus with 1 tablespoon oil and ¼ teaspoon each salt and pepper. Roast until just tender, 8 to 12 minutes; transfer to platter.
2. Meanwhile, in small bowl, combine vinegar, shallot and ¼ teaspoon each salt and pepper. Let sit, tossing occasionally, until asparagus is done.
3. Stir remaining tablespoon oil into shallot mixture, then gently toss with mint and feta. Spoon over asparagus and sprinkle with dill.
4. AIR FRYING INSTRUCTIONS:
5. Heat air fryer to 400°F. Toss asparagus with 1 tablespoon olive oil and 1/4 teaspoon each salt and pepper. Air-fry, shaking basket halfway through, until tender, 10 minutes. Proceed with steps 2-3.

Crispy Parmesan Potato Wedges

Servings: 2

Ingredients:
- 2 small russet potatoes
- 2 tablespoons (28 grams) Parmesan cheese, grated
- ¾ teaspoon (4 grams) salt
- ¼ teaspoon (2 grams) garlic powder
- ¼ teaspoon (2 grams) paprika
- ¼ teaspoon (2 grams) dried oregano
- 1 tablespoon (15 milliliters) neutral-flavored oil

Directions:
1. Cut each potato lengthwise into 8 wedges and place them in a large bowl.
2. Add the remaining ingredients and toss to coat.
3. Place the crisper plate into the Smart Air Fryer basket, then place the potatoes onto the crisper plate.
4. Select the Fries function, adjust time to 22 minutes, and press Start/Pause.
5. Remove the potato wedges when done and serve.

Air Fryer Roasted Garlic

Servings: 1/2
Cooking Time: 10 Minutes

Ingredients:
- 3 full bulbs garlic
- 1-2 tablespoons olive oil
- 1 teaspoon salt

Directions:
1. Preheat air fryer to 400 F
2. Carefully slice the tops off the garlic bulbs; the cloves inside should be exposed.
3. Drizzle the olive oil over top of each garlic bulb, making sure all the cloves get covered.
4. Sprinkle salt on each bulb and tightly wrap each in tin foil.
5. Place garlic into your air fryer and cook for 18-20 minutes, or until garlic is tender.
6. Allow to cool until you can handle and remove the bulbs from the papery skin.

Air Fryer Garlic Knots

Servings: 6
Cooking Time: 8 Minutes

Ingredients:
- 1 can store-bought pizza dough 13.8 ounces or two cans of thin crust pizza 8 ounces each
- 4 tablespoons unsalted butter melted
- 1/4 cup parmesan cheese grated
- 2 cloves garlic minced
- 1 tablespoon dried parsley flakes
- 1 teaspoon Italian Seasoning

Directions:
1. Open the can of premade pizza dough and on a lightly floured surface, roll it out into a rectangle.
2. With a pizza cutter or kitchen knife cut the dough into twelve 1-inch strips, and then fold each strip in half. Tie each piece into dough knots, making 12 knots.
3. Place the dough balls into the air fryer basket in a single layer, lined with parchment paper, a silicone baking mat or lightly sprayed with olive oil spray.
4. Air fry at 350 degrees F for 8-10 minutes, until they are golden brown.
5. While knots are in a small mixing bowl, stir together the melted butter, parmesan cheese, garlic, parsley flakes, and Italian seasoning.
6. When knots are golden brown, use a pastry brush and generously brush garlic butter on each piece with butter and seasonings and top with grated parmesan cheese.

NOTES

Kitchen Tips: Make these in batches without overcrowding the basket. Use a food scale to ensure they are all the same size, so they cook evenly. To get a deeper brown color cook for 1 additional minute.

If using regular crust dough, knots will be just a tad bit thicker and may need 1-2 additional minutes of air frying time.

For smaller bites, just cut the dough in half, and you will have 24 garlic knots.

Optional Favorite Dipping Sauce: Our favorite sauce for dipping is marinara. But you can use other sauces, like homemade marinara sauce, alfredo sauce, pesto sauce, pizza sauce or Greek yogurt with roasted garlic.

Artichoke Wings With Vegan Ranch Dip
Servings: 6

Ingredients:
- Artichoke Wings
- One 16-ounce jar marinated artichoke hearts
- 1½ cups all-purpose flour
- 1 teaspoon garlic powder
- 1 teaspoon onion powder
- 1 teaspoon paprika
- 1 teaspoon kosher salt
- One 12-ounce bottle beer (Lager or Weisse-style for best results)
- 2 cups panko breadcrumbs
- Vegan Ranch Dip
- 1 cup vegan mayonnaise
- ¼ cup non-dairy milk (i.e., coconut, oat, or any nut milk)
- 2 tablespoons fresh dill, finely chopped
- 1 teaspoon fresh Italian parsley leaves, finely chopped
- 1 teaspoon vegan Worcestershire sauce (optional)
- 1 teaspoon apple cider vinegar
- 1 teaspoon lemon juice
- 1 clove garlic, grated
- 1 teaspoon onion powder
- 1 teaspoon black pepper
- Kosher salt, to taste
- Oil spray

Directions:
1. Select the Preheat function on the Air Fryer then press Start/Pause.
2. Drain the artichoke hearts and pat dry with paper towels.
3. Whisk together the flour, garlic powder, onion powder, paprika, and salt in a large bowl until evenly distributed.
4. Pour in the beer and whisk well until no lumps remain. The mixture should resemble pancake batter.
5. Place the panko breadcrumbs in a separate medium bowl.
6. Line the preheated air fryer baskets with parchment paper.
7. Dredge the artichoke hearts in the beer batter, then roll in the panko breadcrumbs.
8. Shake off any excess breadcrumbs, then place the dredged artichoke hearts into the lined air fryer baskets.
9. Spray the wings lightly with oil and insert into the preheated air fryer.
10. Adjust temperature to 400°F and time to 10 minutes, press Shake, then press Start/Pause.
11. Flip the wings and spray again halfway through cooking. The Shake Reminder will let you know when.
12. Combine all the dressing ingredients in a separate medium bowl and whisk together.
13. Season to taste with kosher salt. Pour into a bowl for dipping.
14. Remove the artichoke wings from the air fryer when done.
15. Serve immediately with the vegan ranch dressing.

Air Fryer Sweet Potato Casserole
Servings: 6
Cooking Time: 10 Minutes

Ingredients:
- 29 ounce sweet potato yams drained
- 3/4 cup pecans
- 1/4 teaspoon salt
- 1 egg
- 1/2 teaspoon vanilla extract
- 1/4 teaspoon ground cinnamon
- 1 1/4 cup granulated white sugar
- 1 Tablespoon heavy cream
- 2 Tablespoons unsalted butter softened

Directions:
1. Preheat the air fryer to 350 degrees Fahrenheit.
2. Place the sweet potatoes into a medium sized mixing bowl. Add the salt, butter, egg, vanilla extract, ground cinnamon, white sugar, and heavy cream. Mix thoroughly for one minute.

3. Place the pecans in a food processor. Chop the pecans until they are small and easy to sprinkle.
4. Take the sweet potato mixture and place in a prepared 7" springform pan. Cover the top with the chopped pecans.
5. Place the springform pan into the air fryer basket. Air fry for 10-12 minutes or until the topping is browned.

NOTES

Can I make a sweet potato casserole in the air fryer with a marshmallow topping?

Yes, you can, but you may want to consider doing it a little differently than the traditional method of topping the casserole with mini marshmallows. Because marshmallows are light and fluffy, they can easily blow around and possibly blow up into the heating element. If you want to have a marshmallow topping, consider using the jarred marshmallow fluff, or push the marshmallows into the casserole so that they don't fly around while air frying.

How do I store leftover sweet potato casserole?

Store leftover sweet potato casserole in an airtight container in the refrigerator for up to 4 days.

How do I reheat leftover air fryer sweet potato casserole?

To reheat leftover casserole, add it to an oven-safe dish and reheat in the air fryer at 350 degrees Fahrenheit for 2-3 minutes, or until the casserole is heated through.

What are additions I can make to sweet potato casserole?

You can change the flavors in sweet potato casserole by adding different ingredients such as diced pineapple. It gives the casserole an even more pronounced flavor and it is delicious!

Air Fryer Diced Potatoes

Servings: 4
Cooking Time: 20 Minutes

Ingredients:
- 1 ½ pounds of small potatoes
- 2 cups cold water
- 1 tablespoon fresh thyme or 1 teaspoon dried thyme
- ½ tablespoon minced garlic
- ½ tablespoon olive oil
- Juice of 1/2 a lemon, about 2 tablespoons of a medium size lemon
- Salt to taste

Directions:
1. Wash your potatoes and dice them into small cubes. The closer they are in size, the more evenly they will cook.
2. Soak the cut potatoes for 10 minutes in cold water. This will help remove some starch and allow them to crisp up more. Once they have soaked, drain them and then pat them dry with a paper towel.
3. Combine potatoes with the thyme, garlic, olive oil and lemon juice.
4. Place diced potatoes in your air fryer basket. Cook at 380 degrees F for 20 to 25 minutes, giving the basket a good shake at the 10 minute mark.

NOTES

HOW TO REHEAT DICED POTATOES IN THE AIR FRYER

Preheat the air fryer to 350 degrees F.

Lay the leftover diced potatoes in the air fryer basket in a single layer.

Cook for 3 to 5 minutes until heated through.

Air Fryer Kielbasa

Servings: 4
Cooking Time: 8 Minutes

Ingredients:
- 1 package Kielbasa 15 ounces

Directions:
1. To make this kielbasa dish, remove sausage from packaging, and then cut into bite-size pieces (about ½ inch sized coin size pieces.)
2. Transfer to the air fryer basket, and air fry at 380 degrees F for 8-10 minutes. I tossed the pieces of sausage halfway through air frying.
3. Remove from basket and serve!

NOTES

How to Air Fry Frozen Kielbasa

If you want to make this from frozen, place it in the air fryer basket, and air fry at 380 degrees F, for 10-12 minutes cooking time.

SNACKS & APPETIZERS RECIPES

Air Fryer Green Bean Fries

Servings: 4
Cooking Time: 5 Minutes

Ingredients:
- 1 pound green beans fresh
- 1 cup Parmesan cheese
- 1 cup panko bread crumbs
- 1 Tablespoon garlic powder
- 2 eggs
- 1/2 cup all purpose flour
- 2 Tablespoons Olive oil spray

Directions:
1. Preheat Air Fryer to 390 degrees Fahrenheit (199 degrees Celcius).
2. Snap the ends off the fresh green beans, then place them into a colander to rinse. Place the green beans on a paper towel and pat dry.
3. Coat the green beans in the all purpose flour.
4. Whisk together the eggs in a small bowl.
5. Mix together parmesan cheese, panko breadcrumbs, and garlic powder in a separate bowl.
6. Dip the green beans into the egg mixture, and then dip the green beans into the panko and cheese mixture.
7. Coat the green beans well. Add the green beans to a cooling rack as you work to finish the remainder of the green beans. Spray the coated beans with a light coating of olive oil.
8. Place the coated green beans in the Air Fryer basket and air fry for 5 minutes or until golden brown.
9. Sprinkle with additional parmesan cheese or fresh lemon juice if desired and serve with your favorite dipping sauce.
10. NOTES
11. Arrange your green beans in a single layer: Spreading your green beans out ensures even cooking through the dish.
12. Cooking spray: You can use olive oil cooking spray, canola oil spray, or avocado oil spray for this recipe.
13. Coat the green beans well: Use a bit of the breading mix when coating your green beans. The more breading you have, the crispier your green beans will be.
14. This recipe was made with a basket-style 5.8 qt Cosori Air Fryer. If you're using a different brand, you may have to adjust your cooking time accordingly.

Frozen Waffle Fries In The Air Fryer

Servings: 4
Cooking Time: 8 Minutes

Ingredients:
- 1 pound frozen waffle fries (1/2 bag)
- OPTIONAL
- Dipping sauce of choice

Directions:
1. Preheat your air fryer to 400 degrees F.
2. Place a single layer of frozen waffle fries in your air fryer. They can overlap slightly.
3. Cook the fries for 8 to 10 minutes, carefully shaking the basket halfway through cooking.
4. Remove the waffle fries from the air fryer, serve with your favorite dipping sauce, and enjoy!
5. NOTES
6. HOW TO REHEAT WAFFLE FRIES IN THE AIR FRYER:
7. Preheat your air fryer to 350 degrees.
8. Place your leftover waffle fries in the air fryer and cook for about 2 minutes, until warmed thoroughly.

Blistered Snap Peas

Servings: 4

Ingredients:
- 1 lb. snap peas, strings removed
- 2 tbsp. olive oil
- 1/2 to 1 teaspoon gochugaru
- Kosher salt
- 1/2 lemon, plus wedges for serving
- Cilantro, for serving

Directions:
1. Place grill basket on grill and heat grill and basket, covered, on high 10 minutes.

2. In large bowl, toss snap peas with oil, gochugaru, and 1/2 teaspoon salt. Add to grill basket and grill, tossing twice, until charred and just tender, 5 to 8 minutes.
3. Squeeze juice of 1/2 lemon on top and toss to combine. Transfer to shallow bowl or platter and serve with additional wedges and sprinkle with cilantro if desired.

AIR FRYER DIRECTIONS:
Heat air fryer to 400°F. In large bowl, toss snap peas with oil, gochugaru and 1/2 teaspoon salt. Add snap peas to air-fryer basket and air-fry until slightly charred and just tender, 5 to 6 minutes. Squeeze juice of lemon half on top. Using tongs, quickly toss to combine, then transfer snap peas to shallow bowl or platter. Serve with lemon wedges and sprinkle with cilantro.

Air Fryer Cinnamon Sugar Tortilla Chips
Servings: 2
Cooking Time: 6 Minutes

Ingredients:
- 2 flour tortillas 6 inch
- 1/4 cup granulated sugar
- 1 tablespoon unsalted butter melted
- 1 teaspoon ground cinnamon

Directions:
1. In a medium bowl, combine the sugar and cinnamon, stirring together. Set cinnamon sugar mixture aside.
2. Lay tortillas flat, and then brush the top of each tortilla with melted butter.
3. Sprinkle cinnamon sugar over tortillas until well coated. Use a pizza cutter and slice tortillas into triangles.
4. Place them in a single layer into the air fryer basket lined with a sheet of parchment paper.
5. Air fry at 350 degrees F for 6-8 minutes, or until they reach desired crispness. Shake basket halfway through the cooking process.
6. Remove chips and place them on a wire rack to cool and remain crispy.

NOTES

Optional Dessert Dips: Fresh fruit salsa, marshmallow cream, melted chocolate, strawberry sauce, caramel cinnamon apple dip or cream cheese fruit dip.
Optional Additional Toppings: Fresh strawberries, vanilla ice cream, whipped cream or chocolate shavings.
Cooking Tips: You will definitely want to make a double batch of these tasty treats. Tortilla pieces can slightly overlap if needed.

Air Fryer Tortilla Chips
Servings: 4
Cooking Time: 6 Minutes

Ingredients:
- 4 corn tortillas small
- 1 tablespoon olive oil
- 1/2 tsp salt

Directions:
1. Using a pastry brush, or oil spray, brush or spray a light coating of oil onto the tortilla triangles.
2. Use a pizza cutter or sharp knife and cut the tortillas into triangles.
3. Place tortilla wedges into the air fryer basket, laying them in a single layer, without overlap.
4. Sprinkle tortilla pieces with salt or other seasonings you may wish to use.
5. Working in batches, air fry at 350 degrees Fahrenheit for 7-9 minutes, turning the chips halfway through cooking time. Chips will be golden brown and crispy when done.

NOTES
When air frying, remember that the cook time may vary depending on type of air fryer, and size and type of tortilla pieces. If using larger tortillas, cooking time may need to be adjusted by a couple minutes.
Placing the tortilla slices in a single layer helps them to cook evenly and become crispy.
For additional flavors, you can use additional spices and seasonings. A few bolder flavors you can add would be: curry powder ,white cheddar popcorn powder, or a light sprinkle of chili powder.

You can also add a simple boost of flavor by adding garlic powder, cinnamon, a dash of lime juice and then season with salt before air frying.

Air Fryer Green Beans
Cooking Time: 8 Minutes

Ingredients:
- 1 lb Green beans (trimmed)
- 6 cloves Garlic (minced)
- 1/2 tsp Sea salt
- 1/4 tsp Black pepper
- 2 tbsp Olive oil
- 1 tbsp Lemon juice

Directions:
1. Preheat the air fryer to 375 degrees F (191 degrees C).
2. In a large bowl, combine all the ingredients.
3. Arrange green beans in the air fryer basket, in a single layer.
4. Cook green beans in the air fryer for 7-10 minutes, until tender. Shake the basket halfway through the cook time.

Air Fryer Pasta Chips
Servings: 6
Cooking Time: 20 Minutes

Ingredients:
- 8 ounces rigatoni pasta or bow tie or penne (I used tortiglioni)
- 1 Tablespoon olive oil
- ¼ cup freshly shredded Parmesan cheese plus extra for garnish if desired
- 1 teaspoon Italian dressing mix or your favorite seasoning mix (or ½ teaspoon oregano and ½ teaspoon garlic powder)
- ¼ teaspoon kosher salt
- ¼ teaspoon freshly ground black pepper
- parsley finely chopped, to garnish, optional

Directions:
1. Cook pasta to al dente according to package directions. Do not overcook. Drain and return to the pot to remove moisture.
2. About 2 minutes before pasta is ready, preheat air fryer to 400°F.

3. Add olive oil, parmesan, and seasoning to the pot of pasta, toss to coat.
4. Add pasta to air fryer basket* and cook for 10-12 minutes**, tossing the basket every 3-4 minutes until they are cooked to desired doneness.
5. Cool for about 3-4 minutes before serving. Garnish with parsley and parmesan if desired. Serve with dip, salsa, or hummus.

Notes
*While a single layer is best (meaning you may need to do batches), tossing the basket every 3-4 minutes works to cook them all at once!
**The "pasta chips" crisp as they cool. If you'd like them to be a bit more crisp after they've cooled, simply pop them back in the air fryer for another couple of minutes.

Air Fryer Potato Chips
Servings: 4

Ingredients:
- 4 large Russet Potatoes
- 1 tbsp olive oil
- 1 tsp salt

Directions:
1. Wash the potatoes and pat dry.
2. Use a mandolin slicer or sharp knife and slice the potatoes into ⅛ inch slices.
3. Place the potato slices in a medium bowl of water. Let them soak for at least 30 minutes. The water will get cloudy as they soak.
4. After they have soaked, drain potatoes and rinse them again in cold water and pat dry with a paper towel.
5. Toss the potato slices in the olive oil, and season with salt. Working in batches, place the slices in a single layer in the air fryer basket.
6. Set your oven to Air Frying at 380 degrees F. Cook for 10-15 minutes, depending on the thickness of the cut. Shake the basket halfway through cook time. Cook the chips until they begin to turn golden brown.
7. Remove the chips and place them on a sheet of paper towels until they cool. Garnish with fresh parsley flakes or season with salt to taste.

Air Fryer Kale Chips

Servings: 4
Cooking Time: 3 Minutes

Ingredients:
- 1 bunch kale
- 2 teaspoons olive oil
- 1/2 teaspoon salt

Directions:
1. Wash the kale and pat dry until completely dry. Roughly tear the leaves into bite sized pieces.
2. Add the kale to a mixing bowl, then drizzle with olive oil. Using your hands, rub the leaves to ensure they have some oil on them. Sprinkle the salt all over.
3. Transfer the kale to the air fryer basket and air fry at 190C/375F for 3-4 minutes, ensuring they don't burn.
4. Repeat the process until all the kale chips are cooked.

Notes

TO STORE: It's best to store the cooled kale chips in a paper bag at room temperature to prevent them from becoming soggy. They should stay crisp for up to 3 days.

Air-fryer Cheesy Mozzarella Chips

Servings: 6
Cooking Time: 10 Minutes

Ingredients:
- 2 tbs plain flour
- 2 tsp onion powder
- 1/2 tsp garlic salt
- 1/4 tsp ground paprika
- 3 free range eggs
- 1 1/2 cups panko breadcrumbs
- 550g mozzarella
- 5ml olive oil cooking spray
- 1/2 cup basil pesto (to serve)
- 2 sprigs basil, leaves picked (to serve)

Directions:
1. Combine flour, onion powder, garlic salt and paprika in a shallow bowl. Season with pepper. Whisk eggs in a separate shallow bowl. Place breadcrumbs in a separate shallow bowl.
2. Cut mozzarella block in half crossways. Then cut each in half horizontally to form 4 thin pieces. Cut each piece into 5 sticks. Dip mozzarella sticks in flour mixture to coat. Shake off excess. Working in batches, coat mozzarella sticks in egg mixture then in breadcrumbs. Repeat crumbing process to double crumb. Spray the chips with oil after double crumbing.
3. Preheat air fryer to 200°C for 2 minutes. Working in 2 batches, cook mozzarella sticks in air fryer for 4 minutes or until golden. Stand for 2 minutes, then transfer to a board. Top with basil and serve with pesto.

Air Fryer Zucchini Chips

Servings: 4
Cooking Time: 12 Minutes

Ingredients:
- 1 medium zucchini cut into ½" coins
- 1 beaten egg
- cooking spray
- Crumb Coating
- ⅔ cup Panko bread crumbs
- ⅔ cup seasoned bread crumbs
- 2 tablespoons Parmesan cheese grated
- 1 teaspoon Italian seasoning

Directions:
1. Preheat air fryer to 375°F.
2. Mix coating ingredients in a bowl.
3. Toss zucchini with egg. Dip zucchini into the coating mixture gently pressing to adhere.
4. Lightly spray zucchini with cooking spray.
5. Place in a single layer in the air fryer basket and cook 6 minutes. Turn zucchini over and air fry 6-8 minutes more or until crisp and zucchini is tender.

Notes

For batches, undercook zucchini by 2 minutes. Once all batches are cooked, place them all in the air fryer together for 3 minutes to heat through.Reheat in the air fryer at 375°F for 3-5 minutes or until heated through.

Air Fryer Spicy Onion Rings

Servings: 4
Cooking Time: 10 Minutes

Ingredients:
- 2 large sweet onions, sliced 1/2 inch thick
- Batter:
- ⅔ cup buttermilk
- 1 egg
- ¼ cup all-purpose flour
- 1 teaspoon RedHot Chile and Lime Seasoning Blend (such as Frank's®)
- ½ teaspoon adobo all-purpose seasoning (such as Goya®)
- Breading:
- 2 cups panko bread crumbs
- 1 teaspoon adobo all-purpose seasoning (such as Goya®)
- ½ teaspoon RedHot Chile and Lime Seasoning Blend (such as Frank's®)
- olive oil cooking spray
- 1 teaspoon kosher salt, or to taste

Directions:
1. Whisk together buttermilk, egg, flour, chile and lime seasoning, and adobo seasoning for the batter in a shallow bowl. Cover and refrigerate for 30 minutes.
2. Combine panko, adobo seasoning, and chile and lime seasoning in a shallow dish; mix well. Remove batter from the fridge. Dip onion rings first into the batter, then into bread crumb mixture, turning to coat, and gently shake off excess crumbs. Lightly spritz the onion rings with cooking spray on both sides.
3. Preheat the air fryer to 340 degrees F (170 degrees C). Line the air fryer basket with a parchment liner or lightly spray with oil.
4. Place the breaded onion rings into the fryer basket in an even layer, leaving about 1/2-inch space between the slices.
5. Cook until crisp and lightly browned, flipping halfway through, 10 to 12 minutes. You may have to cook in batches, and cooking time may vary depending on the size and brand of your air fryer.
6. Remove from the air fryer, transfer to a baking sheet, sprinkle with kosher salt, and

place in a 250 degrees F (120 degrees C) oven to keep warm.
7. Cook's Notes:
8. You can find Chile n' Lime seasoning and Adobo seasoning in the Hispanic section of your supermarket. Adobo should be available at most stores, but if Chile n' Lime is not, use all Adobo.
9. Chilling the batter will make the breading adhere better. You may bread the onion rings, cover early in the day, and refrigerate until ready to cook.

Easy Onion Rings

Servings: 2
Cooking Time: 10-30 Minutes

Ingredients:
- 1 large onion, sliced into rings about 1.5cm/⅝in thick
- 4 tbsp plain flour
- 1 free-range egg
- 1 tbsp milk (dairy or unsweetened non-dairy)
- 60g/2¼oz panko breadcrumbs
- cooking oil spray
- salt and freshly ground black pepper

Directions:
1. Preheat the oven to 200C/180C Fan/Gas 6, or the air fryer to 180C.
2. Carefully separate the onion slices into rings; some rings should be one onion-layer thick, others two layers.
3. Put half the flour in a shallow bowl and season with salt and pepper. Put the remaining flour in another shallow bowl and whisk in the egg and milk to make a smooth batter. Put the panko breadcrumbs in another shallow bowl.
4. Dip the onion rings into the seasoned flour, making sure they are thoroughly coated all over. Lightly tap off excess flour. Put the floured rings into the batter and flip a few times to coat completely, shaking off excess batter. Finally add them to the breadcrumbs and press crumbs all over them.
5. Spray a baking sheet or the inside of your air fryer with cooking oil. Add the onion rings

in a single layer – if air frying you'll need to do them in batches. Spray the tops of the onion rings with more oil.

6. Bake in the oven for 18–20 minutes, turning after 8–10 minutes. Air-fry for 10 minutes, turning halfway through. Keep the first batches of air fryer onion rings warm in a low oven while you cook the rest, then serve immediately.

Air Fryer Beet Chips

Servings: 4
Cooking Time: 30 Minutes

Ingredients:
- 3 beets
- 1 Tablespoon olive oil
- 1 teaspoon Kosher salt
- 1 teaspoon ground black pepper

Directions:
1. Carefully peel the beets and then slice them to your desired thickness using a mandolin. (Careful, these are sharp!)
2. Add the sliced beets into a medium sized mixing bowl and then coat with olive oil, salt, and pepper. Mix until the beets are coated evenly.
3. Add the beet chips in a single layer into the basket of the air fryer. It's ok to overlap the beet chips slightly.
4. Air fry beet chips at 320 degrees Fahrenheit for 30 minutes, carefully flipping the beef chips halfway through the cooking process.
5. Start checking on the chips with 5 minutes remaining and pull the chips early if they are browning fast. (This will depend on the size and thickness of the slices.)
6. Remove the beet chips for the air fryer basket and place them on a wire cooling rack for a few minutes before serving.

NOTES
This recipe was made with a 1700 watt basket style 5.8 quart Cosori air fryer. If you are using a different size or different brand of air fryer, you may need to add a minute or two. All air fryers cook a little differently.
Store any leftover beet chips in an airtight container for up to 3 days.

Consider spicing things up by adding a ¼ teaspoon of cayenne pepper, white pepper, or even some red pepper flakes.

Air-fryer Healthier Veggie Chips

Servings: 4
Cooking Time: 1 Hr 30 Minutes

Ingredients:
- 1 large washed white potato, cut into 1mm-thick slices
- 300g beetroot, trimmed, cut into 1mm-thick slices
- 150g carrot, trimmed, cut into 1mm-thick slices
- 1 1/2 tbs Woolworths extra virgin olive oil
- 1 sprig rosemary, leaves picked, finely chopped

Directions:
1. Place potato in a medium bowl and cover with cold water. Stand for 15 minutes to soak. Place beetroot and carrot in separate bowls. Add 2 tsp oil to beetroot and carrot bowls and toss to coat.
2. Preheat air fryer to 180°C for 2 minutes. Working in 4 batches, cook beetroot and carrot for 15 minutes, shaking basket every few minutes, or until golden and crisp.
3. Drain potatoes, pat dry with a clean tea towel. Transfer to a dry bowl, add remaining oil and toss to coat. Working in 2 batches, cook potato for 15 minutes, shaking basket every few minutes, or until golden and crisp. Sprinkle chips with rosemary to serve.

Air Fried Cheesy Mashed Potato Balls

Ingredients:
- Leftover mashed potatoes
- 1 cup cheese of your choice
- 1 cup green chiles
- Auntie NoNo's Everything Seasoning
- 1/2 cup Flour
- 2 eggs

- 1 cup Panko breadcrumbs

Directions:
1. If you aren't using leftover mashed potatoes, you will need to refrigerate them until they are cold.
2. Add in the cheese, green chiles and a generous amount of Auntie Nono's Everything seasoning to the potatoes and mix until well combined.
3. Preheat the air fryer oven to 350°.
4. Prepare your breading station by putting flour, 2 whisked eggs and the panko bread crumbs in 3 separate bowls and set aside.
5. Using an ice cream scooper, scoop the potatoes into medium sized balls.
6. Dip the balls into the flour, then the egg and lastly, into the bread crumbs.
7. Arrange them all onto the mesh rack accessory and air fry at 350° for 8-9 minutes.
8. Dip these in your favorite dipping sauce and enjoy!

Air Fryer Keto Onion Rings Recipe
Servings: 4
Cooking Time: 16 Minutes

Ingredients:
- 1 large Onion (sliced into rings 1/2 inch thick)
- 3 tbsp Wholesome Yum Coconut Flour
- 1/4 tsp Sea salt
- 2 large Eggs
- 2/3 cup Pork rinds (~1.8 oz)
- 3 tbsp Wholesome Yum Blanched Almond Flour
- 1/2 tsp Paprika
- 1/2 tsp Garlic powder

Directions:
1. Arrange 3 small, shallow bowls in a line:
2. Coconut flour and sea salt, stirred together
3. Eggs, beaten
4. Pork rinds, almond flour, paprika, and garlic powder, stirred together
5. Lightly grease 2 air fryer oven racks or an air fryer basket.

6. Dredge an onion ring in coconut flour. Dip it in the egg, shake off the excess, then place in the pork rind mixture. Scoop extra pork rind mixture over it, so that it's coated on all size. Place into the air fryer rack or basket. Repeat with all the onion rings, placing them in a single layer without touching. (You may need to cook them in two batches if you don't have 2 air fryer racks.)
7. Preheat the air fryer or air fryer oven to 400 degrees F for 2 to 3 minutes.
8. For an air fryer oven: Place both racks into the air fryer oven. Bake for about 8 minutes, until the top layer is golden. Switch racks and bake for 8 more minutes, until the top layer is golden again.
9. For a regular air fryer: Only half the onion rings will fit into the basket in a single layer. Place the basket into the air fryer. Bake for 16 minutes, until golden. Remove the onion rings, arrange the next batch of uncooked rings, and repeat.

Air Fryer Turnip Fries
Servings: 4
Cooking Time: 15 Minutes

Ingredients:
- 1 tbs olive oil
- 500g turnips, peeled and sliced into fries
- 1/2 tsp garlic powder
- 1/2 tsp smoked paprika

Directions:
1. Add the turnip fries, olive oil and seasonings to a large bowl and toss well to coat.
2. Place in the air fryer basket and cook for 8 minutes at 200°C, toss and cook for 5 minutes more, until crisp.

Air Fryer Sweet Potato Fries
Servings: 4
Cooking Time: 15 Minutes

Ingredients:
- 2 medium sweet potatoes
- 1 tablespoon olive oil
- 1/2 teaspoon fine sea salt

- 1/2 teaspoon garlic powder
- 1/4 teaspoon paprika

Directions:
1. Cut sweet potatoes into 1/2 inch strips to create fries.
2. Coat sweet potato fries with olive oil.
3. Add in the fine sea salt, garlic powder, and paprika and mix to combine seasoning evenly.
4. Cook the sweet potato fries at 380 degrees for 15-18 minutes, shaking the basket every 5 minutes.

NOTES
HOW TO REHEAT SWEET POTATO FRIES IN THE AIR FRYER:
Preheat your air fryer to 350 degrees.
Place your leftover sweet potato fries in the air fryer and cook for about 3 to 5 minutes, until warmed and crisped.

Air Fryer Seasoned French Fries
Servings: 4
Cooking Time: 15 Minutes

Ingredients:
- 4 Russet Potatoes peeled, cut into strips
- 1 tbsp olive oil
- 2 tsp paprika
- 1 tsp kosher salt
- 1 tsp garlic powder
- 1 tsp onion powder
- 1 tsp red pepper flakes
- 1/2 tsp black pepper
- 1/4 tsp cayenne pepper

Directions:
1. Peel, and rinse the potatoes.
2. Using a mandolin slicer or sharp knife, cut the potatoes into strips about ¼ inch in thickness.
3. In a medium bowl, soak the strips of potato in cold water for about 30 minutes, then drain them, and pat them dry with a paper towel.
4. Pour in the olive oil and seasonings, tossing the fries to coat them.
5. Place the fries in the air fryer basket, in a single layer, and cook at 400 degrees F for 15-20 minutes, until they are crispy. Shake the basket halfway through cooking.

Homemade Chips
Servings: 4

Ingredients:
- 500g white potatoes, cut in 6mm thick by 5cm long sticks
- 1/2-3 tbsp vegetable oil
- COOKING MODE
- When entering cooking mode - We will enable your screen to stay 'always on' to avoid any unnecessary interruptions whilst you cook!

Directions:
1. Soak cut potatoes in cold water for 30 minutes to remove excess starch. Drain well, then pat with a paper towel until very dry
2. Place both ingredients into a large mixing bowl; toss to combine. Use at least 1/2 tablespoon oil. For crispier results, use up to 3 tablespoons oil
3. Insert crisper plate in pan and pan in unit. Preheat unit by selecting AIR FRY, setting the temperature to 200°C and setting the time to 3 minutes. Select START/STOP to begin
4. After 3 minutes, place chips on the crisper plate; reinsert pan. Select AIR FRY, set temperature to 200°C and set time to 25 minutes. Select START/STOP to begin
5. After 10 minutes, remove pan from unit and shake chips or toss them with silicone-tipped tongs. Reinsert pan to resume cooking
6. Check chips after 20 minutes. For crispier chips, continue cooking for up to 25 minutes
7. When cooking is complete, serve immediately with your favourite sauce

Crispy Air Fryer Potato Chips

Servings: 4
Cooking Time: 50 Minutes

Ingredients:
- 1 medium russet potato (about 12 ounces)
- 1 tablespoon canola oil
- 1/2 teaspoon kosher salt, plus more for seasoning
- Cooking spray

Directions:
1. Using a mandoline or sharp knife, cut 1 medium russet potato crosswise into very thin slices (about 1/8th-inch thick). Transfer to a large bowl and add enough ice water to cover. Soak for 20 minutes.
2. Drain the potatoes well. Spread them out in a single layer on a double layer of paper towels to dry. Let dry for 10 minutes. Wipe the bowl dry.
3. Heat an air fryer to 370°F. Meanwhile, return the potato slices to the bowl. Add 1 tablespoon canola oil and 1/2 teaspoon kosher salt and toss until evenly combined.
4. Coat the air fryer basket with cooking spray. Add enough potato slices to sit in a single, even layer. Air fry until golden brown and crispy, shaking the basket or rotating the trays or flipping the chips every 4 minutes, 15 to 18 minutes total.
5. Carefully transfer the chips with a slotted spoon or tongs to a serving plate or bowl. Repeat air frying the remaining chips, patting them dry before air frying if needed. Season with more kosher salt while warm.

RECIPE NOTES
Storage: Air fryer potato chips are best eaten the day they are made. Leftovers can be stored in an airtight container at room temperature and reheated in the air fryer for 2 minutes to re-crisp.

Air Fryer Ravioli

Servings: 4-6

Ingredients:
- 2 large eggs
- 2 tbsp. whole milk
- 1 c. Italian bread crumbs
- 1/4 c. grated Parmesan, plus more for serving
- 1/4 tsp. kosher salt
- Freshly ground black pepper
- 1 (20-oz.) package refrigerated ravioli
- Cooking spray
- Pesto or marinara, for serving

Directions:
1. In a shallow bowl, whisk eggs and milk. In another shallow bowl, combine bread crumbs and Parmesan; season with salt and a few grinds of pepper.
2. Working one at a time, dip ravioli into egg mixture, then into bread crumb mixture, pressing to adhere. Dip back into egg mixture. Place on a plate.
3. Lightly coat an air-fryer basket with cooking spray. Working in batches, arrange ravioli in basket, spacing about 1/4" apart; spray with cooking spray. Cook at 400°, flipping halfway through and spraying with cooking spray, until golden and cooked through, about 7 minutes.
4. Arrange ravioli on a platter. Top with more Parmesan. Serve warm with pesto alongside for dipping.

VEGETABLE & & VEGETARIAN RECIPES

Air Fryer Squash

Servings: 4
Cooking Time: 7 Minutes

Ingredients:
- 1 medium summer squash or zucchini
- ½ teaspoon Italian seasoning
- 1 tablespoon olive oil
- salt & pepper to taste

Directions:
1. Slice squash or zucchini into ½" slices.
2. Toss with olive oil and seasonings.
3. Preheat air fryer to 400°F.
4. Add squash and cook 6-7 minutes or until tender crisp. Cook for 2 minutes longer if you prefer a softer squash.

Air Fryer Asparagus

Servings: 4
Cooking Time: 7 Minutes

Ingredients:
- 1 pound asparagus
- 1 tablespoon olive oil
- salt and pepper to taste

Directions:
1. Preheat the air fryer to 400°F.
2. Wash and dry the asparagus trimming the ends*.
3. Toss the asparagus with the oil and seasonings.
4. Place in the air fryer basket and cook for 7-10 minutes or until tender.

Notes
To trim the ends: Hold the stalk and bend it until the thick end snaps off (about 1 to 2 inches from the end). Line up the remaining stalks and cut them to the same length.

Air Fryer Mushrooms And Onions

Servings: 2

Ingredients:
- 2 cloves garlic, minced
- 2 tbsp. extra-virgin olive oil
- 4 tsp. fresh lemon juice, plus 1/4 tsp. finely grated lemon zest for serving
- 1 tsp. kosher salt
- 1 tsp. Worcestershire sauce
- 1 lb. baby bella or button mushrooms, halved, quartered if large
- 1 small yellow onion, halved and thinly sliced
- 1 tbsp. chopped fresh parsley
- 1 tbsp. fresh thyme leaves

Directions:
1. In a large heatproof bowl, whisk garlic, oil, lemon juice, salt, and Worcestershire to combine. Add mushrooms and onion and toss until oil mixture is completely absorbed by mushrooms (this will take about 30 seconds).
2. Working in batches if necessary, in an air-fryer basket, spoon mushroom mixture in a single layer; reserve bowl. Cook at 400°, tossing a few times to ensure even cooking, until mushrooms and onions are tender and golden, 13 to 15 minutes.
3. Return hot mushroom mixture to reserved bowl. Toss with parsley, thyme, and lemon zest.

Keto Fried Pickles

Servings: 4
Cooking Time: 7 Minutes

Ingredients:
- 9 large pickles sliced lengthways
- 3/4 + 1 tablespoon almond flour
- 1/2 teaspoon salt
- 1/4 teaspoon pepper
- 1 cup parmesan cheese
- 2 large eggs
- 2 tablespoons sour cream

Directions:
1. Slice your dill pickles lengthways and set aside.
2. In a small bowl, add your almond flour, salt, pepper, and parmesan cheese and mix until combined. In a separate bowl, whisk together the eggs and sour cream.

3. Dip the dill pickles in the wet mixture, followed by the dry mixture. Repeat the process until all the pickles are battered.
4. Add some oil to a non-stick pan. Once hot, add the battered pickles to it and fry for 3-4 minutes, flipping halfway through, until golden brown.
5. Serve the fried pickles immediately with your favorite condiments.

Notes

If you'd like to make this in an air fryer, simply prepare as instructed. Once ready to cook, add them to an air fryer basket and air fry at 200C/400F for 8 minutes.

TO STORE: Leftover pickles should be stored in the refrigerator, covered, for up to three days.

TO FREEZE: Place the cooked and cooled pickles in an airtight container and store them in the freezer for up to two months.

REHEAT: As the fried pickles are 'battered', they should not be microwaved. Instead, reheat them in the air fryer or in a preheated oven.

Air Fryer Roasted Potatoes

Servings: 4
Cooking Time: 20 Minutes

Ingredients:
- 24 oz petite potatoes
- 1 tbsp olive oil
- 1/2 tsp onion powder
- 1/2 tsp garlic powder
- 1/4 tsp smoked paprika
- 1/4 tsp white pepper
- 1/2 tsp ground black pepper

Directions:
1. Take the potatoes and place them in a colander. Rinse well.
2. Use a knife and cut the petite potatoes in half down the center.
3. Add the cut potatoes to a medium sized mixing bowl. Coat with olive oil and seasonings. Stir well to coat.
4. Add the seasoned potatoes to the basket of the prepared air fryer basket.
5. Cook the potatoes at 400 degrees Fahrenheit for 10 minutes.

6. Open the air fryer and shake the basket. Continue to cook for an additional 6-10 minutes.
7. Remove the roasted potatoes from the air fryer and top them with fresh parsley before serving.

NOTES

Every air fryer is different so if you have a stronger powered air fryer, you may need to cut the time a little to ensure you don't overcook the potatoes. I personally find that 16-17 minutes for small petite potato halves in my Cosori 5.8 is perfect. However, you may need to add additional time depending on the size of your potatoes and the brand of air fryer you use.

Air Fryer Cauliflower

Servings: 4
Cooking Time: 13 Minutes

Ingredients:
- 1 head cauliflower florets
- 1 tablespoon olive oil
- salt and pepper to taste

Directions:
1. Preheat the air fryer to 390°F.
2. Toss the cauliflower with oil and seasonings in a large bowl.
3. Place in the air fryer basket and cook for 12-13 minutes, shaking the basket halfway through cooking.

Notes

Store leftover cauliflower in an airtight container in the fridge for up to 4-5 days. Reheat in the air fryer or under the broiler until crispy.

Air Fryer Potato Wedges

Servings: 4
Cooking Time: 25 Minutes

Ingredients:
- 3 small russet potatoes* about 1 1/2 pounds
- 2 tablespoons extra-virgin olive oil
- 1 teaspoon kosher salt plus a few pinches
- 1/2 teaspoon garlic powder optional
- 1 teaspoon chili powder optional

Directions:

1. Scrub the potatoes (leave the peels on). Cut each in half lengthwise, then cut lengthwise again to make quarters. Cut each quarter such that you end up with 1/2-inch wedges (likely you'll be cutting each quarter into thirds depending upon your potato). You will have about 12 or so wedges per potato.
2. Place the wedges in a large bowl. Fill the bowl with cool water, swish the potatoes around, then pour off the water. Repeat once or twice more, until the water runs clear (this removes the starch from the potatoes and helps them crisp). Once you've rinsed the potatoes, pour very hot tap water over the top so that it covers the potatoes by at least 1 inch. Let sit 10 minutes. Do not skip rinsing or soaking or the fries will not be as crisp.
3. Spread the potato wedges onto a clean towel and pat very dry. Dry out the bowl you used to rinse them, then return the potatoes to the bowl. Top the potatoes with the oil, salt, garlic powder, and chili powder and toss to coat.
4. Preheat your air fryer to 350 degrees F. Add all of the potato wedges to the air fryer basket (it's OK if that they're overlapping; that's the beauty of this method).
5. Air fry the potato wedges for 10 minutes, then use tongs to gently but thoroughly toss and redistribute them. Continue to air fry at 350 degrees F for 5 minutes more.
6. Gently toss and turn the potatoes once more, then increase the air fryer temperature to 400 degrees F. Continue air frying until the potato wedges are crisp, about 15 minutes more, tossing the potatoes every 5 minutes and checking them fairly often towards the end to ensure then do not burn.
7. Transfer the wedges to a serving plate and sprinkle lightly with additional salt. Enjoy immediately.

Notes

*If possible, use potatoes that are 5-inches or less in length; longer ones still work, but they tend to break when tossed in the air fryer.

TO STORE: Place leftover air fryer potato wedges in an airtight storage container in the refrigerator for up to 3 days.

TO REHEAT: Reheat leftover potato wedges in the air fryer at 375 degrees F and recrisp for a few minutes.

TO FREEZE: Freeze potato wedges in a single layer on a baking sheet until solid. Transfer the frozen fries to an airtight, freezer-safe storage container or ziptop bag for up to 3 months. Reheat from frozen.

Air Fryer Egg-fried Vegetable Rice

Servings: 2
Cooking Time: 15 Minutes

Ingredients:

- 1½ tbsp light soy sauce
- 3 eggs, lightly beaten
- 4 salad onion, timmed and sliced
- 1½ tbsp sesame oil
- 2 clove/s garlic, finely chopped
- 1 red chilli, sliced
- 210g pack Bright & Colourful Ginger Stir Fry (or similar-sized pack of stir fry vegetables)
- 15g ginger, peeled and finely chopped (if not included in the vegetable stir fry pack above)
- 250g Waitrose brown basmati rice 250g
- Sweet chilli sauce, to serve (optional)

Directions:

1. Turn the air fryer to 180°C and remove the grate from the cooking bowl. Combine ½ tbsp soy sauce with the eggs and sliced salad onions. Add ½ tbsp sesame oil to the hot bowl of the air fryer and immediately pour in the egg mixture. Cook for 2 minutes, then stir and cook for a further minute. Transfer to a plate and set aside.
2. Drizzle in the remaining 1 tbsp oil, then add the garlic, chilli, stir fry vegetables (except the coriander, if included) and ginger, if using. Stir well and cook for 4-5 minutes, until the veg has begun to turn golden in places.
3. Stir in the rice with the remaining 1 tbsp soy sauce, breaking it up with a spatula and folding it through the softened vegetables.

Continue to cook for about 6 minutes, stopping to stir every 2 minutes, until the vegetables are just cooked and the rice is piping hot. Stir the eggs through for the final 2 minutes. Serve in warm bowls, scattered with any reserved coriander leaves and some sweet chilli sauce, if liked.

NOTES

Customer safety tips

Follow manufacturer's instructions and advice for specific foods

Pre-heat the air fryer to the correct temperature

If cooking different foods together, be aware that they may require different times and temperatures

Spread food evenly – do not overcrowd pan/chamber

Turn food midway through cooking

Check food is piping/steaming hot and cooked all the way through

Aim for golden colouring – do not overcook

Air Fryer Blooming Onion

Servings: 4

Ingredients:
- FOR THE ONION
- 1 large yellow onion
- 3 large eggs
- 1 c. breadcrumbs
- 2 tsp. paprika
- 1 tsp. garlic powder
- 1 tsp. onion powder
- 1 tsp. kosher salt
- 3 tbsp. extra-virgin olive oil
- FOR THE SAUCE
- 2/3 c. mayonnaise
- 2 tbsp. ketchup
- 1 tsp. horseradish
- 1/2 tsp. paprika
- 1/2 tsp. garlic powder
- 1/4 tsp. dried oregano
- Kosher salt

Directions:
1. Slice off onion stem and set onion on flat side. Cut an inch from the root down, into 12 to 16 sections, being careful not to cut all the way through. Flip over and gently pull out sections of onion to separate petals.
2. In a shallow bowl, whisk together eggs and 1 tablespoon water. In another shallow bowl, whisk together breadcrumbs and spices. Dip onion into egg wash, then dredge in breadcrumb mixture, using a spoon to fully coat. Drizzle onion with oil.
3. Place in basket of air fryer and cook at 375° until onion is tender all the way through, 20 to 25 minutes. Drizzle with more oil as desired.
4. Meanwhile make sauce: In a medium bowl, whisk together mayonnaise, ketchup, horseradish, paprika, garlic powder, and dried oregano. Season with salt.
5. Serve onion with sauce, for dipping.

Air Fryer Butternut Squash

Servings: 4
Cooking Time: 16 Minutes

Ingredients:
- 1 butternut squash cubed
- 1 tablespoon olive oil
- 2 teaspoons minced garlic or 1 teaspoon garlic powder
- 1/2 tsp salt or to taste
- 1/4 tsp pepper or to taste

Directions:
1. To make this easy air fryer recipe, use a sharp vegetable peeler and peel the butternut squash skin. Use a sharp chef knife, and cut squash halves, lengthwise, and then remove all seeds.
2. Cut the squash into cubes about the size of dice. I try to do 1-inch cubes. You can skip the steps if you use pre-cut butternut squash cubes.
3. In a medium mixing bowl, add the butternut squash cubes, and toss squash with olive oil and seasonings.
4. Once pieces of squash are well coated, in a single layer, pour seasoned squash pieces into the air fryer basket or onto baking sheet for a rack air fryer.
5. Cook butternut squash on Air Fry, at 400 degrees for 16 to 18 minutes cook time,

until squash is crispy and tender to your liking. Shake the basket halfway during the cooking process.
6. Season cooked squash with additional salt and pepper to taste. Garnish with fresh parsley if desired.

NOTES

If using a larger squash, cook in two batches so the squash is not too stacked or overlapping while cooking.

Because all air fryer are different, cooking times may vary.

Air Fryer Brussels Sprouts

Servings: 4
Cooking Time: 12 Minutes

Ingredients:

- FOR THE BRUSSELS SPROUTS:
- 1 pound Brussels sprouts
- 2 teaspoons extra virgin olive oil
- 1/4 teaspoon kosher salt
- 1/4 teaspoon black pepper
- 3 cloves garlic thinly sliced (optional but delish!)
- OPTIONAL TOPPINGS:
- 1 tablespoon balsamic glaze or reduced balsamic vinegar
- Drizzle pomegranate molasses
- 2 teaspoons pure maple syrup
- 3 tablespoons freshly grated Parmesan cheese

Directions:

1. Trim off the ends of the Brussel sprouts and remove any brown outer leaves. Cut them in half from stem to end. If any are very large, cut them into quarters from stem to end so that all the pieces are fairly similar in size and cook evenly.
2. OPTIONAL—This step makes sure the Brussels sprouts a little more tender in the middle; that said, if you don't mind a firmer sprout, you can skip it—I like my Brussels sprouts firm/tender inside and crispy outside, so I typically skip it—Place the Brussels sprouts in a large bowl and cover with warm tap water. Let sit 10 minutes.
3. Preheat the air fryer to 375 degrees, according to the manufacturer's instructions (for my air fryer, that's 3 minutes of preheating).
4. Drain the Brussels sprouts and with a towel, lightly pat dry. Wipe out the bowl you used for soaking, then add the Brussels sprouts back to it (if you didn't soak the sprouts, simply place them in a large mixing bowl). Drizzle with the oil and sprinkle with the salt and black pepper. Toss to coat evenly, then add them to your fryer basket.
5. Cook the sprouts for 5 minutes, then slide out the basket and shake it to toss the Brussels sprouts to promote even cooking. Cook 5 additional minutes, then slide out the basket again. The Brussels sprouts should look like they are getting nice and crispy and are almost done (if not, let them cook a minute or so longer). Add the garlic cloves and toss to coat once more. Cook 2 to 4 additional minutes, checking and shaking the basket often, until the Brussels sprouts are deeply crisp.
6. If adding toppings, transfer the Brussels sprouts to a serving bowl (or wipe out the mixing bowl you previously used) and stir in any desired toppings. Enjoy hot.

Notes

TO STORE: Refrigerate Brussels sprouts in an airtight storage container for up to 4 days.

TO REHEAT: Rewarm leftovers on a baking sheet in the oven at 350 degrees F.

TO FREEZE: The Brussels sprouts will get mushy once thawed, so I don't recommend freezing them. If you have lots leftover, you can freeze them in an airtight freezer-safe storage container for up to 3 months. Let thaw overnight in the refrigerator before reheating.

Air Fryer Buffalo Cauliflower Wings

Servings: 6
Cooking Time: 25 Minutes

Ingredients:

- 1 cup superfine almond flour , can sub with gluten-free oat flour if not grain-free
- 1/4 cup finely crushed grain-free crackers or crushed pork rinds if you are not plant-based. , optional for extra crispy wings
- 1/2 cup unsweetened almond milk , can sub with any milk of choice
- 1 tsp onion salt , we like the one from Trader Joe's
- 1 tsp paprika
- 1/2 tsp garlic powder
- 4 cups cauliflower florets , about 1 medium cauliflower
- 1/2 cup buffalo sauce (Tessamae's, Primal Kitchen, OR Frank's)
- 3 Tbs vegan butter , can sub with Ghee if not dairy-free for Whole30

Directions:

1. Cut the Cauliflower into pieces: Remove most of stem and chop the cauliflower into even bite-sized pieces.
2. Make the Batter: In a large bowl, combine almond flour, almond milk ,onion salt, garlic powder and paprika in a bowl and mix until smooth.
3. Add the cauliflower florets to the mixture and toss to coat.
4. Air Fryer:
5. Place the cauliflower florets into a single layer in air fryer basket, working in batches as needed.
6. Air Fry at 375 for 12-14 minutes until golden brown, shaking halfway through.
7. Meanwhile, mix the hot sauce & melted vegan butter / ghee together in a bowl.Pour the buffalo sauce evenly over the cauliflower & toss to coat. Air Fry for an additional 2-3 minutes or until crispy and just starting to brown.
8. Air Fry for an additional 2-3 minutes or until crispy and just starting to brown.
9. Serve and garnish with fresh chopped herbs, if desired and serve with your favorite dipping sauce.
10. Oven:
11. Preheat oven to 400 degrees F and line a baking pan with parchment paper.
12. Place florets in a single layer on baking sheet.
13. BAKE for 20-25 minutes until golden brown, flipping halfway through.
14. Meanwhile, mix the sauce ingredients together.
15. Take the cauliflower out of the oven and dip each wing into the sauce, or coat with a pastry brush or you can pour the sauce evenly over the cauliflower & toss to coat.
16. Place the pan back into the oven for 5-7 minutes or until crispy and just starting to brown.
17. Serve and garnish with fresh chopped herbs, if desired and serve with your favorite dipping sauce.

NOTES
*Feel free to add other spices you like.

Simple Air Fryer Brussels Sprouts

Servings: 6
Cooking Time: 15 Minutes

Ingredients:

- 1 ½ pounds Brussels sprouts
- 2 tablespoons olive oil
- 1 teaspoon garlic powder
- 1 teaspoon salt
- ½ teaspoon ground black pepper

Directions:

1. Preheat an air fryer to 390 degrees F (200 degrees C) for 15 minutes.
2. While the air fryer is preheating, trim Brussels sprouts. Place in a bowl with olive oil, garlic powder, salt, and pepper in a bowl and mix well. Spread sprouts evenly in the air fryer basket.
3. Cook in the preheated air fryer for 15 minutes, shaking the basket halfway through the cycle.

Air Fryer Corn On The Cob

Servings: 4
Cooking Time: 10 Minutes

Ingredients:
- 4 ears corn on the cob
- 1 tablespoon olive oil
- 4 tablespoons butter for serving, optional
- salt & pepper optional

Directions:
1. Preheat the air fryer to 400°F.
2. Brush the corn with olive oil and cook 10-12 minutes, turning occasionally.
3. While corn is cooking, melt butter. Brush butter over the corn and season with salt & pepper to taste.

Notes

Preheat the air fryer before adding the corn.

Peel the corn and rinse any silk and dab them dry before brushing with oil.

Corn can be cooked in batches and kept warm using the warm setting or setting the air fryer to 170°F.

The easiest way to butter corn is to melt the butter and brush it with butter.

Quick & Easy Air Fryer Asparagus

Servings: 4
Cooking Time: 7-9 Minutes

Ingredients:
- 1 pound medium to thick asparagus
- 1 teaspoon olive oil
- 1/4 teaspoon kosher salt
- 1/4 teaspoon freshly ground black pepper

Directions:
1. Heat an air fryer to 400°F or 425°F (choose the higher temperature if available). Meanwhile, trim the woody ends from 1 pound asparagus. Transfer to a medium bowl, add 1 teaspoon olive oil and 1/4 teaspoon kosher salt, and toss to coat.
2. Add the asparagus to the air fryer and spread into a single layer. Air fry until the asparagus is tender and slightly crispy on the ends, stopping to shake the basket (or rotate the pans in larger air fryers) about halfway through, 8 to 10 minutes total.

Transfer to a serving platter and sprinkle 1/4 teaspoon black pepper evenly over the top.

NOTES

Storage: Refrigerate leftovers in an airtight container for up to 4 days.

Mexican Street Corn

Servings: 4
Cooking Time: 12 Minutes

Ingredients:
- 4 ears corn, husks and silks removed
- 1 cup Mexican crema
- 2 limes, zested and juiced
- ½ cup cotija cheese, finely crumbled
- ⅓ cup cilantro, finely chopped
- 2 tablespoons chile de arbol powder or other chili powder
- Items Needed:
- Empty squeeze bottle with lid
- Funnel (optional)

Directions:
1. Place the cooking pot into the base of the Smart Indoor Grill, followed by the grill grate.
2. Select the Air Grill function on max heat, adjust time to 12 minutes, press Shake, then press Start/Pause to preheat.
3. Place the corn onto the preheated grill grate, then close the lid.
4. Flip the corn halfway through cooking. The Shake Reminder will let you know when.
5. Place the crema and lime juice in a medium bowl and stir until well combined, then transfer into the squeeze bottle. Place the cap onto the squeeze bottle and then set aside until ready to use.

Note: Using a funnel may help transferring the crema to the squeeze bottle.Remove the corn when done and place onto a platter.

Use the squeeze bottle to apply the crema to the top of the corn, then sprinkle the lime zest, cotija cheese, cilantro, and chile powder over the top and serve.

Air Fryer Broccoli And Cauliflower

Servings: 4
Cooking Time: 8 Minutes

Ingredients:
- 2 cups broccoli florets cut into bite size pieces
- 2 cups cauliflower florets cut into bite size pieces
- 2 tablespoons extra virgin olive oil
- 1 teaspoon garlic powder
- 1/2 teaspoon kosher salt

Directions:
1. In a large bowl, add fresh broccoli and fresh cauliflower.
2. Then add in olive oil, garlic powder, and salt, tossing together until vegetables are well coated.
3. Spray olive oil spray into the basket to make sure vegetables get crispier edges and do not stick.
4. Pour vegetables into the air fryer basket. Air fry at 380 degrees F for 8-10 minutes until the vegetables have crisp edges and are golden brown.
5. Toss or shake the basket halfway through the cooking process.
6. Serve while hot.

NOTES

Optional Additional Toppings: Fresh lemon juice and zest, sautéed bell peppers, sprinkle of parmesan cheese, lemon zest or creamy cheese sauce.

Cooking Tips: You can cut and season the florets in advance which makes meal prep even easier. Precut florets can be found in the produce section of your local grocery store, just be sure and cut larger pieces so every piece is bite size.

Substitutions: Use refined coconut oil, avocado oil or vegetable oil in place of olive oil.

Oven Baked Buffalo Cauliflower

Servings: 8
Cooking Time: 30 Minutes

Ingredients:
- 1 head of cauliflower washed and dried
- 1 cup milk
- 1 cup flour
- 1 tablespoon olive oil
- 1 teaspoon garlic powder
- pepper to taste
- ⅔ cup Panko bread crumbs
- ⅔ cup buffalo sauce (see note below)

Directions:
1. Preheat oven to 450°F.
2. Cut cauliflower into bite-sized pieces and discard the core.
3. Combine milk, flour, oil, garlic powder, and pepper in a large bowl. Place batter and cauliflower in a large zippered bag and gently toss until cauliflower is coated.
4. Pour cauliflower into a large strainer, letting any excess batter drip off. You want just a light coating of batter. Sprinkle with Panko breadcrumbs and gently toss.
5. Place on a foil-lined pan and bake for 15 minutes. Remove from the oven and gently toss with buffalo sauce. You want the cauliflower coated but not soaked.
6. Place cauliflower back on the pan and bake for an additional 5-10 minutes or until cauliflower is tender-crisp.
7. Serve with ranch or blue cheese dressing.

Notes

Note: You can purchase store-bought buffalo sauce or mix ⅓ cup melted butter with ⅔ cup hot sauce (such as Frank's Red Hot). Whisk until combined.

Ensure the cauliflower is very dry after washing. You can use a salad spinner or shake it dry. I try to wash it the day before if I can.

Toss the cauliflower in the wet batter and let most of the excess drip off, you want just a light coating.

Gently add some of the buffalo sauce to the cauliflower, you don't want them saturated with sauce or they will get soggy.

If some of your friends/family don't like spice, leave a few aside when adding buffalo sauce and season with salt and black pepper instead. Serve them with your favorite dips.

Air Fryer Tofu

Servings: 4
Cooking Time: 10 Minutes

Ingredients:

- 15 oz tofu extra firm
- 1/2 tablespoon olive oil
- 1/2 tablespoon sesame oil
- 2 tablespoons soy sauce
- 1/2 teaspoon garlic powder
- 1/2 teaspoon ground ginger
- 1/4 teaspoon salt

Directions:

1. Preheat the air fryer to 190C/375F.
2. Cube the tofu into bite sizes pieces. Place the tofu on a dishtowel or paper towel to soak up excess moisture.
3. In a large bowl, combine the olive oil, sesame oil, soy sauce, garlic powder, and salt. Add the tofu and mix well, until all the tofu is coated.
4. Generously grease the air fryer basket and add a single layer of tofu to it. Air fry for 10-12 minutes, shaking the basket several times throughout.
5. Once the tofu is golden brown, remove it from the basket and repeat the process until all the tofu is cooked up.

Notes

TO STORE: Store leftover crispy tofu in an airtight container in the fridge for up to 4 days.
TO REHEAT: To reheat air-fried tofu, preheat the air fryer to 375F degrees. Add tofu to the air fryer basket and cook for a few minutes until heated through.
TO FREEZE: You can also freeze air-fried tofu if you have made a big batch. Flash-freeze tofu and transfer it into an airtight bag or container. Keep cooked tofu in the freezer for up to 3 months.

Air Fryer Herbed Brussels Sprouts

Servings: 4
Cooking Time: 8 Minutes

Ingredients:

- 1 lb. brussels sprouts (cleaned and trimmed)
- ½ tsp. dried thyme
- 1 tsp. dried parsley
- 1 tsp. garlic powder (Or 4 cloves, minced)
- ¼ tsp. salt
- 2 tsp. oil

Directions:

1. Remove any outer leaves of the brussels sprouts that don't look healthy. Lightly cook your brussels sprouts, either by boiling them for 13-15 minutes or by microwaving them on high for about 3-4 minutes.
2. Cut them in half.
3. Place all ingredients in a medium or large mixing bowl and toss to coat the brussels sprouts evenly.
4. Pour them into the food basket of the air fryer and close it up.
5. Set the heat to 390 F. and the time to 8 minutes. This setting roasts them nicely on the outside while leaving the insides a nicely cooked al dente.
6. Cool slightly and serve.

Notes
Please note that the nutrition data below is a ballpark figure. Exact data is not possible.

Air Fryer Cauliflower 'wings'

Servings: 4
Cooking Time: 10-30 Minutes

Ingredients:

- 1 small–medium cauliflower, cut the cauliflower into florets, approx. 4–6cm/1½–2½in, save the stalk and leaves for another recipe
- 125g/4½oz plain flour
- 1 tsp baking powder
- 1 tsp paprika
- cooking oil spray
- 2–3 tbsp buffalo hot sauce (check that it's vegan)
- salt and freshly ground black pepper
- For the dip
- 175g/6oz unsweetened oat-based yoghurt
- 1 small garlic clove, crushed or finely grated
- 1 lemon, zest only, plus juice of ½ lemon
- 3 tbsp finely chopped fresh herbs, such as coriander, chives, dill, mint – or a mix

Directions:
1. Preheat the air fryer to 200C.
2. Put the flour, baking powder and paprika in a bowl with some salt and pepper. Whisk in 150ml/¼ pint cold water to make a thick batter. Dip the cauliflower florets in to coat them and set aside on a plate.
3. Spray the air fryer basket with oil, then add the florets in a single layer (they can be touching: you can break them apart after cooking). Spray the tops with more oil and air-fry for 10 minutes, or until golden brown and crispy but cooked through. (You may need to cook in two batches.)
4. Meanwhile, make the dip. Mix the yoghurt, garlic, lemon zest and juice together in a bowl, then stir in the chopped herbs and season to taste.
5. If you cooked the cauliflower in batches, put all the florets back into the air fryer and heat for 1 minute.
6. Put 2 tablespoons of the hot sauce into a big bowl. Tip in the hot cauliflower florets and mix to coat all of the pieces. Serve immediately, drizzled with the third tablespoon of hot sauce if you dare, and the cooling dip alongside.

NOTES

This recipe was made in an air fryer without a paddle attachment. The batter needs to set on the cauliflower until it is crisp before it will come away from the air fryer basket.

No air fryer? Preheat the oven to 200C/180C Fan/Gas 6. Line a baking sheet with baking paper, spray with cooking oil and bake the battered cauliflower florets for 20 minutes, until crispy.

Air-fryer Asparagus

Servings: 4

Ingredients:
- 1/4 cup mayonnaise
- 4 teaspoons olive oil
- 1-1/2 teaspoons grated lemon zest
- 1 garlic clove, minced
- 1/2 teaspoon pepper
- 1/4 teaspoon seasoned salt

- 1 pound fresh asparagus, trimmed
- 2 tablespoons shredded Parmesan cheese
- Lemon wedges, optional

Directions:
1. Preheat air fryer to 375°. In large bowl, combine the first 6 ingredients. Add asparagus; toss to coat. Working in batches, place in a single layer on greased tray in air-fryer basket.
2. Cook until tender and lightly browned, 4-6 minutes. Transfer to a serving platter; sprinkle with Parmesan cheese. If desired, serve with lemon wedges.

Crispy Air Fryer Brussels Sprouts

Ingredients:
- 1 lb. brussels sprouts, trimmed and halved lengthwise (approximately 4 cups)
- 1 tablespoon olive oil
- 1/2 tablespoon Italian seasoning
- 1/2 tablespoon garlic powder
- 1/8 teaspoon salt
- 1/4 teaspoon ground black pepper, or to taste

Directions:
1. Combine all ingredients in a large bowl and toss to combine and coat brussels sprouts evenly. Transfer brussels sprouts to air fryer basket.
2. Turn air fryer on to 350 F and cook for 12 minutes, until brussels sprouts are cooked through and golden brown on the edges.

NOTES

These instructions work best with a Philips Air Fryer (1.8 lb/2.75 qt). If you have larger or smaller air fryer, you will have to adjust the cook time. Just check in on the brussels sprouts every 5 minutes to make sure that it cooks through and that they don't burn.

Maple Glazed Roasted Vegetables With Pesto And Spiced Nuts

Servings: 4
Cooking Time: 40 Minutes

Ingredients:

- For the vegetables
- 500 g carrots, sliced lengthways then into diagonal chunks (or so evenly sized)
- 500 g parsnips, sliced lengthways then into diagonal chunks (or so evenly sized)
- 200 g brussels sprouts
- 1 red onion
- 2 cloves of garlic, minced
- 4 tbsp maple syrup
- 1 tbsp wholegrain mustard
- 150 g mixed nuts
- 2 tbsp olive oil
- 1 sprig fresh rosemary,
- 1 tsp cayenne
- For the pesto
- 50 g fresh basil leaves
- 2 cloves of garlic, crushed
- 25 g pine nuts
- 40 parmesan, grated
- 4 tbsp olive oil

Directions:

1. For the vegetables
2. In a large bowl, whisk together the 3 tbsp of maple syrup, mustard and 1 tbsp of the olive oil
3. Pre-heat the air fryer to 190 degrees
4. Add the veg to the maple marinade and toss together so all the pieces are coated.
5. Place veggie pieces into the air fryer tray and cook for 15/20 minutes – you may need to do this in batches, around half way through give the air fryer pan a shake or 2 to give an even cook
6. For the pesto
7. Put the basil leaves in a food processor with the garlic and pine nuts Blitz for a few seconds, then add the cheese and oil and blitz again until you have a spoon-able paste.
8. For the nuts
9. Preheat air fryer to 150 degrees
10. In a bowl add the rosemary, cayenne, 1 tbsp oil, 1 tbsp of maple syrup, and the nuts
11. Mix together so all the nuts are coated.
12. Add to tray of the air fryer in one layer and air fry for around 5-8 minutes – about half way give the tray a shake.
13. Once cool, arrange the dish of the veggies, drizzle of pesto and a sprinkling of the spiced nuts – and serve up!

Air-fryer Crispy Tofu Recipe

Servings: 2
Cooking Time: 17 Minutes

Ingredients:

- 280g pack The Tofoo Co extra firm tofu, drained and cut into 1-2cm cubes
- 1 tbsp cornflour
- ¼ tsp white pepper
- pinch chilli flakes
- 1 tsp sesame seeds
- 1 tsp vegetable oil
- chopped fresh coriander, to serve (optional)
- chopped fresh coriander, to serve (optional)
- 1 tbsp runny honey
- 1 tsp rice wine vinegar
- 1 clove garlic, crushed

Directions:

1. Preheat the air-fryer to 200°C.
2. Pat dry the drained tofu and put into a bowl. Sprinkle over the cornflour, white pepper, chilli flakes and sesame seeds and season with salt and black pepper. Toss well until coated, then drizzle over the oil, tossing to coat.
3. Put the tofu pieces into the air-fryer, well-spaced. Cook for 15 mins, shaking every 5 mins, until golden and very crisp.
4. For the sauce, put all the ingredients into a heat-safe bowl and microwave for 1-2 mins, stirring regularly, until steaming. Mix well and set aside to cool. Serve alongside the crispy tofu bites or drizzle over and toss to glaze if you prefer.

FAVORITE AIR FRYER RECIPES

Air Fryer Elote

Servings: 4
Cooking Time: 10 Minutes

Ingredients:

- Corn
- 4 ears of corn on the cob shucked and cleaned
- 2 tablespoons olive oil separated
- 1/2 teaspoon salt separated
- 1/2 teaspoon ground black pepper
- Elote Sauce
- ½ cup plain Greek yogurt
- 2 tablespoons mayo
- 2 oz. cotija cheese crumbled
- 1 tablespoon fresh lime juice
- 1 tablespoon lime zest
- ¼ teaspoon cayenne pepper

Directions:

1. Preheat the air fryer to 350°F. Drizzle the 4 ears of corn with 1 tablespoon of olive oil. Massage the oil into the corn with your hands. Season the corn with ½ teaspoon of salt and ½ teaspoon of pepper.
2. Add 1 tablespoon of olive oil to the bottom of the air fryer and then transfer the corn to the air fryer. Cook the corn for 10 minutes, flipping halfway.
3. While the corn is cooking, add all of the ingredients (except for the cayenne pepper) for the elote sauce to a bowl and mix to combine. Pour the sauce on a large plate. Spread the sauce out evenly.
4. Remove the corn from the air fryer and roll each ear of corn in the elote sauce. Use a spoon to drizzle more elote sauce over the corn. Then season the corn with the cayenne pepper. Enjoy!
5. Air fryer elote on a plate.

Tips & Notes

Every air fryer is different, so the cook time may vary slightly.

If cayenne pepper is too spicy, replace it with ground paprika.

Air Fryer Mini Corn Dogs

Servings: 4
Cooking Time: 8 Minutes

Ingredients:

- 20 mini corn dogs frozen
- toppings Ketchup, mustard

Directions:

1. Place the mini corn dogs into the air fryer basket, without stacking or overlapping. If you have a smaller basket, air fry 10 at a time.
2. Air fry at 380 degrees F for 9-11 minutes, or until corn dogs reach your desired crispness and the hot dog in the middle is cooked.
3. Serve with your favorite toppings.

NOTES

I make this recipe in my Cosori 8 qt. air fryer or 6.8 quart air fryer. Depending on your air fryer, size and wattages, cooking time may need to be adjusted 1-2 minutes.

Air Fryer Flatbread Pizzas

Servings: 2
Cooking Time: 10 Minutes

Ingredients:

- 2 pre-cooked flatbread or naan
- 1/2 cup (120 ml) pizza sauce or tomato sauce
- 1/3 cup (40 g) shredded cheese
- salt , to taste
- black pepper , to taste
- OPTIONAL TOPPINGS
- Pepperoni, cooked Sausage, Bacon pieces, diced Ham, sliced or diced Tomatoes, Mushrooms, Pineapple, etc.
- OTHER SAUCE OPTIONS
- BBQ Sauce, Salsa, White (Alfredo) Sauce, Pesto, etc.
- EQUIPMENT
- Air Fryer
- Air Fryer Rack optional

Directions:

1. Place the flatbreads (naan) in air fryer bottom side up (make sure it is in just a single layer - cook in batches if needed).
2. Air Fry at 360°F/182°C about 2-3 minutes. Flip the flatbreads over. Continue to Air fry at 360°F/182°C for another 1-2 minutes (if you want the crust extra crispy - air fry each side a couple minutes more).
3. Divide the sauce between the toasted flatbreads. Top with cheese and add additional salt, pepper and other preferred toppings.
4. To keep your topping from flying around, place an air fryer rack over the flatbread pizzas.
5. Air Fry the pizzas at 360°F/182°C for 2-5 minutes or until heated through and cheese is melted.

Air Fryer Pita Pizzas
Servings: 1
Cooking Time: 10 Minutes
Ingredients:
- 1 pita bread
- 2 Tablespoons (30 ml) pizza sauce or tomato sauce
- 1/4 cup (28 g) shredded cheese
- salt , to taste
- black pepper , to taste
- OPTIONAL TOPPINGS
- Pepperoni, cooked Sausage, Bacon pieces, diced Ham, sliced or diced Tomatoes, Mushrooms, Pineapple, etc.
- OTHER SAUCE OPTIONS
- BBQ Sauce, Salsa, White (Alfredo) Sauce, Pesto, etc.
- EQUIPMENT
- Air Fryer
- Air Fryer Rack optional

Directions:
1. Place the pita in air fryer (if making multiple pita pizzas, make sure it is in just a single layer - cook in batches if needed). Air Fry at 360°F/182°C for 2 minutes.
2. Flip the pita bread over. Continue to Air fry at 360°F/182°C for another 1-2 minutes (if

you want the crust extra crispy - air fry each side a couple minutes more).
3. Spread the sauce over the toasted pita bread. Top with cheese and add additional salt, pepper and other preferred toppings.
4. To keep your topping from flying around, place an air fryer rack over the pita pizzas.
5. Air Fry the pizzas at 360°F/182°C for 2-5 minutes or until heated through and cheese is melted. Allow to cool for a couple minutes, then slice and serve warm.

Char Siu Dinner
Servings: 5
Ingredients:
- Marinade:
- 1 teaspoon five-spice powder
- 2 teaspoons kosher salt
- ¼ teaspoon ground white pepper
- 4 tablespoons granulated sugar
- 1½ tablespoons soy sauce
- 2 tablespoons hoisin sauce
- 1 tablespoon Chinese rice wine
- 2 tablespoons honey
- 2 garlic cloves, minced
- 2 cubes red fermented bean curd, mashed
- 3 teaspoons red fermented bean curd liquid
- Pork:
- 2 pounds Boston butt (pork shoulder), tops and sides scored
- 3 tablespoons honey
- Oil spray
- For Serving:
- 2 cups short grain white rice, steamed
- 1 cup Taiwanese cabbage, sauteed, for serving
- Items Needed:
- Pastry brush

Directions:
1. Combine marinade ingredients in a large bowl and mix until well combined. Set 4 tablespoons of marinade aside in the refrigerator.
2. Remove the thick, fatty pork rinds from around the entire piece of pork shoulder.
3. Slice the pork into smaller pieces, about 2-cm long and ¾-inch thick.

4. Place the pork and marinade into a large resealable plastic bag and shake until fully coated. Marinate for 1-2 days in the refrigerator.
5. Rest the pork for 30 minutes at room temperature before cooking.
6. Select the Preheat function on the Air Fryer, adjust temperature to 400°F, and press Start/Pause.
7. Mix the honey, 1½ tablespoons of water, and the 4 tablespoons of reserved marinade in a small bowl to make a basting mixture.
8. Spray the inner basket of the air fryer with oil spray.
9. Brush both sides of the pork slices with the basting mixture, then place into the preheated air fryer.

Note: The pieces pork can be touching each other, but should not be stacked on top of each other. You may need to work in batches. Set temperature to 400°F and time to 12 minutes, press Shake, then press Start/Pause.

Flip the pork pieces over and brush more of the basting mixture on each side halfway through cooking. The Shake Reminder will let you know when.

Remove the pork when done, then transfer to a wire rack.

Baste the top of the pork with the remaining basting mixture.

Serve the Char Siu over steamed white rice with a side of sautéed Taiwanese cabbage.

Air Fryer French Bread Pizzas
Servings: 2
Cooking Time: 10 Minutes

Ingredients:
- 1 French bread loaf
- 1/2 cup (120 ml) pizza sauce or tomato sauce
- 1/3 cup (40 g) shredded cheese
- salt , to taste
- black pepper , to taste
- OPTIONAL TOPPINGS
- Pepperoni, cooked Sausage, Bacon pieces, diced Ham, sliced or diced Tomatoes, Mushrooms, Pineapple, etc.

- OTHER SAUCE OPTIONS
- BBQ Sauce, Salsa, White (Alfredo) Sauce, Pesto, etc.
- EQUIPMENT
- Air Fryer
- Air Fryer Rack optional

Directions:
1. Cut French bread loaf to fit the length of your air fryer. Slice in half lengthwise.
2. Lightly spray both sides for an extra crispy crust. Place in air fryer basket/tray with the bottom (crust) side up (only cook in a single layer - cook the pizzas in batches if needed). Air Fry at 360°F/182°C about 2 minutes.
3. Flip the bread, add sauce & toppings.
4. Cover toppings with an air fryer rack to keep toppings from flying around.
5. Air Fry 360°F/182°C for 2-4 minutes or until heated through and cheese is melted. Try air frying for about 2 minutes first. If you want the top to be crispier, add additional minute or two until the pizza is crispy and cheese is melted.
6. Allow pizza to cool for about 2 minutes. Serve warm.

Air Fryer Chili Cheese Dogs
Servings: 2
Cooking Time: 5 Minutes

Ingredients:
- 2 hot dogs
- 2 sausage rolls
- 1/2 cup canned or homemade chili of choice warmed or at room temperature
- 1/2 cup shredded cheddar cheese*

Directions:
1. Preheat your air fryer to 400 degrees.
2. Place the hot dogs inside the air fryer and cook for 4 minutes, turning halfway through.
3. Remove the hot dogs from the air fryer and place inside sausage rolls. Gently place each one in the air fryer and add half of the cheddar cheese evenly on top of the hot dogs.

4. Add the chili and then top with the remaining cheddar cheese.
5. Turn air fryer to 350 degrees and cook for 1-2 minutes until cheese has melted and chili is warm.
6. Carefully remove the chili cheese dogs from the air fryer and enjoy immediately.

NOTES

*Mexican cheese can be substituted for cheddar cheese

If cooking hot dogs from frozen:

Place small slits on hot dogs using a knife. Cook on 350 (preheated) for 7-8 minutes until hot dog is heated thoroughly.

Air Fryer Fried Brown Rice

Servings: 2

Ingredients:
- 1 large carrot, peeled, trimmed, and chopped into small pieces (about 3/4 c.)
- 2 scallions, thinly sliced, white and green parts separated
- 2 tsp. finely chopped fresh ginger (from a 1" piece)
- 1 tbsp. vegetable oil
- 1/4 tsp. kosher salt
- 2 c. long-grain brown rice
- 1 clove garlic, finely chopped
- 2 1/2 tsp. low-sodium soy sauce
- 2 tsp. toasted sesame oil
- Freshly ground black pepper
- 1 large egg, lightly beaten
- 1/2 c. frozen peas, thawed

Directions:
1. In a 7" nonstick round pan, combine carrot, white scallion parts, ginger, vegetable oil, and salt. In an air-fryer basket, place pan. Cook at 400°, stirring halfway through, until onion and carrot are just tender, about 5 minutes.
2. Remove air-fryer basket and add rice, garlic, soy sauce, sesame oil, and a few grinds of pepper to carrot mixture; stir to combine. Continue to cook at 400° until rice is lightly toasted, about 5 minutes more.
3. Remove air-fryer basket and pour egg over half of rice mixture and peas over other half.

Continue to cook at 400° until egg is just set and peas are warm, about 4 minutes more; stir to combine. Top with green scallion parts.

Air Fryer Bagel Pizzas

Servings: 2
Cooking Time: 10 Minutes

Ingredients:
- 1 bagel , split in half
- 1/2 cup (120 ml) pizza sauce or tomato sauce
- 1/3 cup (40 g) shredded cheese
- salt , to taste
- black pepper , to taste
- OPTIONAL TOPPINGS
- Pepperoni, cooked Sausage, Bacon pieces, diced Ham, sliced or diced Tomatoes, Mushrooms, Pineapple, etc.
- OTHER SAUCE OPTIONS
- BBQ Sauce, Salsa, White (Alfredo) Sauce, Pesto, etc.
- EQUIPMENT
- Air Fryer
- Air Fryer Rack optional
- Oil Sprayer optional

Directions:
1. Cut the bagels in half and place each half in the air fryer, cut side down (if air frying multiple bagels, only cook in a single layer - cook in batches if needed). Air Fry at 360°F/182°C for 2 minutes.
2. Flip the bagels halves to cut side up. Continue to Air Fry at 360°F/182°C for another 1-2 minutes (if you want the crusts extra crispy - air fry each side an additional minute or two more).
3. Add sauce, toppings, and cheese on top of the bagel halves. Lightly spray with oil for extra crispy.
4. Cover toppings with an air fryer rack to keep toppings from flying around.
5. Air Fry 360°F/182°C for 2-4 minutes or until heated through and cheese is melted. Try air frying for about 2 minutes first. If you want the top to be crispier, add

additional minute or two until the bagel pizzas are crispy and cheese is melted.
6. Allow to cool for about 2 minutes. Serve warm.

Air Fryer Brats
Servings: 6
Cooking Time: 7 Minutes

Ingredients:
- 6 bratwurst uncooked
- 1 serving cooking spray

Directions:
1. Preheat the air fryer to 150C/300F. Spray oil in an air fryer basket.
2. Add the bratwurst in a single layer in the air fryer basket.
3. Cook for 8-10 minutes, flipping halfway through.

Notes
TO STORE: Place leftovers in the refrigerator, covered, for up to 5 days.
TO FREEZE: Place the cooked and cooled brats in a ziplock bag and store it in the freezer for up to two months.
TO REHEAT: Reheat the bratwurst in the microwave, non-stick pan, or air fryer.

Air Fryer Nuts And Bolts
Servings: 4
Cooking Time: 25 Minutes

Ingredients:
- 2 cups dried farfalle pasta
- 60ml (1/4 cup) extra virgin olive oil
- 2 tbsp brown sugar
- 2 tsp smoked paprika
- 1 tsp onion powder
- 1/2 tsp garlic powder
- 1/2 tsp chilli powder
- 1 cup pretzels
- 80g (1/2 cup) raw macadamias
- 80g (1/2 cup) raw cashews
- 1 cup Kellog's Nutri-grain cereal
- 1 tsp sea salt
- Select all ingredients

Directions:

1. Cook pasta in a large saucepan of boiling salted water until just tender. Drain well. Transfer to a tray. Pat dry with paper towel. Transfer to a large bowl.
2. Combine oil, sugar, paprika, onion, garlic and chilli powders in a small bowl. Spoon half of the mixture over pasta. Toss to coat.
3. Preheat air fryer on 200C. Place pasta in air fryer basket. Cook for 5 minutes. Shake basket. Cook for a further 5-6 minutes or until golden and crisp. Transfer to a large bowl.
4. Place pretzels and nuts in a bowl. Add remaining spice mixture. Toss to coat. Place in air fryer basket. Cook on 180C for 3 minutes. Shake basket. Cook for a further 2-3 minutes or until golden. Add to pasta, then add cereal. Sprinkle with salt. Toss to combine. Cool completely. Serve.

Classic Margherita Pizza
Servings: 4

Ingredients:
- Homemade Pizza Dough:
- 1¾ cups bread flour, plus more for kneading
- ½ teaspoon granulated sugar
- 1⅛ teaspoons instant dry yeast
- 1 teaspoon kosher salt
- ¾ cup warm water (90°–110°F)
- 1 tablespoon plus 1 teaspoon olive oil
- Items Needed:
- Stand mixer with dough hook attachment
- Food processor or blender
- Tomato Sauce:
- 1 can peeled whole San Marzano tomatoes (28-ounces)
- 1½ tablespoons extra virgin olive oil
- ½ teaspoon kosher salt
- ¼ teaspoon dried oregano
- Pizza:
- 1 premade pizza dough
- 1 tablespoon olive oil
- 6 tablespoons tomato sauce
- 1.5 ounces fresh mozzarella
- 8–10 fresh basil leaves, roughly torn

Directions:

1. Homemade Pizza:
2. Combine the flour, sugar, yeast, and salt in the bowl of a stand mixer with the dough hook attached and mix on low speed until well combined.
3. Add the warm water and 1 tablespoon olive oil and beat until the dough forms a ball, about 5 minutes.
4. Scrape the dough onto a lightly floured surface and gently knead into a smooth, firm ball.
5. Grease a large bowl with the remaining 1 teaspoon olive oil.
6. Add the dough, cover the bowl, and allow to rise until doubled in size. This will take about 1 hour, depending on the temperature of your kitchen.
7. Turn the dough out onto a lightly floured surface and divide into 2 equal pieces.
8. Cover each with a clean kitchen towel and let rest for 10 minutes before making your pizza.
9. Classic Margherita Pizza:
10. Drain the tomatoes and reserve the liquid.
11. Place the tomatoes, olive oil, salt, and oregano in a food processor or blender and blend until smooth. Season to taste.

Note: Sauce will last 1 week in the refrigerator.Select the Preheat function on the Air Fryer and press Start/Pause.

Stretch out the pizza dough into a 7-inch circle on a floured surface.

Place the pizza dough into the preheated air fryer. Brush the top with 1 tablespoon olive oil.

Set temperature to 400°F and time to 5 minutes, then press Start/Pause.

Flip the pizza dough over when the timer goes off and cook at 400°F for an additional 2 minutes.

Flip the pizza dough back over when the timer goes off and top with 2 to 3 tablespoons tomato sauce. Use the back of a spoon to spread it evenly across the surface, leaving ½-inch of space around the edge of the crust.

Break half of the mozzarella into large pieces and gently place them on top of the sauce.

Cook at 400°F for an additional 5 minutes.

Remove when the dough is golden brown and the cheese is melted.

Top with fresh basil and serve.

Air Fryer Frozen Mozzarella Sticks
Servings: 2
Cooking Time: 6 Minutes

Ingredients:
- 10 frozen mozzarella sticks
- marinara sauce or your favorite dipping sauce

Directions:
1. Preheat the air fryer to 360 degrees.
2. Place the frozen mozzarella sticks in the air fryer cook for 6-8 minutes.
3. Pinch slightly (and carefully since they're hot). They are done when the cheese inside is soft and there is give to the mozzarella stick.
4. Remove them from the air fryer and enjoy with a marinara sauce for dipping.

Air Fryer Totino's Pizza
Servings: 4
Cooking Time: 6 Minutes

Ingredients:
- 1 Totino's Party Pizza

Directions:
1. Remove the frozen pizza from packaging. Lightly spray the air fryer tray or air fryer basket with an air fryer safe cooking spray.
2. Place pizza in basket. No need to preheat air fryer. Air fry at 400 degrees F for 6-8 minutes, until it has a crispy crust and has reached your desired level of crispiness.
3. Serve while hot.

NOTES

I love this brand of frozen pizza because they have options for pizza toppings. I love pepperoni, or triple cheese pizza. Unless the pizza is deep dish, the cooking times should be the same.

Air Fryer Fried Rice

Ingredients:
- 3 cups rice cooked and cold
- 1 cup frozen mixed vegetables
- 1 tbsp oyster sauce
- 1 tsp sesame oil
- 2 eggs scrambled
- 2 tbsp choppled green onion tops

Directions:
1. To make your air fryer fried rice, put your cold rice into an large bowl.
2. Mix in the frozen vegetables to the bowl of rice.
3. Add the scrambled eggs into the rice and vegetables.
4. Add the sesame oil and oyster sauce. Mix well until fully combined.
5. Transfer the rice mixture to an oven safe container like a ramekin.
6. Place that container into your air fryer. Cook the air fried rice at 360 degrees F for 15 minutes stirring every 5 minutes. Add in the green onion tops during the last minutes of cooking time, stirring them in until well combined.
7. Serve immediately.

Air Fryer Tostones
Servings: 2
Cooking Time: 20 Minutes

Ingredients:
- 1 large green plantain (ends trimmed and peeled (6 oz after))
- olive oil spray (I like Bertolli)
- 1 cup water
- 1 teaspoon kosher salt
- 3/4 teaspoon garlic powder

Directions:
1. With a sharp knife cut a slit along the length of the plantain skin, this will make it easier to peel. Cut the plantain into 1 inch pieces, 8 total.
2. In a small bowl combine the water with salt and garlic powder.
3. Preheat the air fryer to 400F.
4. When ready, spritz the plantain with olive oil and cook 6 minutes, you might have to do this in 2 batches.
5. Remove from the air fryer and while they are hot mash them with a tostonera or the bottom of a jar or measuring cup to flatten.
6. Dip them in the seasoned water and set aside.
7. Preheat the air fryer to 400F once again and cook, in batches 5 minutes on each side, spraying both sides of the plantains with olive oil.
8. When done, give them another spritz of oil and season with salt. Eat right away.

Air Fryer Sausage Rolls
Servings: 12
Cooking Time: 10 Minutes

Ingredients:
- Air Fryer Sausage Rolls
- 3 sausages Note 1
- 3 sheets puff pastry
- 1 tbsp sesame seeds
- 1 eggs

Directions:
1. Air Fryer Sausage Rolls
2. Turn the air fryer on to 180°C/350 F for 15 mins
3. Use a knife and chopping board to remove the casing from the sausages
4. Add egg to a small bowl, pierce yoke and whisk
5. Place a sheet of puff pastry (thawed) onto the chopping board and place 1 off the sausages on top
6. Roll the pastry around the sausage, then use a pastry brush to coat the top of the pastry where the 2 bits of pastry will meet
7. Continue to roll the pastry around the sausage and again brush one side of where the pastry joins with the egg
8. Repeat for each sausage
9. Brush the top of the length of the long rolled sausage with egg
10. Sprinkle the top with sesame seeds
11. Use a knife to cut the excess pastry off each end

12. Then cut the long sausage roll into 4 smaller rolls
13. Spray the Air Fryer Basket with oil (or use baking paper) then place raw sausage rolls into Air Fryer (work in batches)
14. Cook sausage rolls in Air Fryer for 7- 9 mins until pastry is golden and crispy
15. Serve with sauce

Air-fryer Nacho Hot Dogs
Servings: 6
Cooking Time: 10 Minutes
Ingredients:
- 6 hot dogs
- 3 cheddar cheese sticks, halved lengthwise
- 1-1/4 cups self-rising flour
- 1 cup plain Greek yogurt
- 1/4 cup salsa
- 1/4 teaspoon chili powder
- 3 tablespoons chopped seeded jalapeno pepper
- 1 cup crushed nacho-flavored tortilla chips, divided
- Cooking spray
- Optional: Guacamole, sour cream and additional salsa

Directions:
1. Cut a slit down the length of each hot dog without cutting through; insert a halved cheese stick into the slit. Set aside.
2. Preheat air fryer to 350°. In a large bowl, stir together flour, yogurt, salsa, chili powder, jalapenos and 1/4 cup crushed tortilla chips to form a soft dough. Place dough on a lightly floured surface; divide into 6 pieces. Roll 1 piece of dough into a 15-in.-long strip and wrap it in a spiral around a cheese-stuffed hot dog. Repeat with remaining dough and hot dogs. Spray wrapped hot dogs with cooking spray and gently roll in remaining crushed chips. Spray air-fryer basket with cooking spray; place hot dogs in basket without touching, leaving room to expand.
3. In batches, cook until dough is slightly browned and cheese starts to melt, 8-10

minutes. If desired, serve with guacamole, sour cream and additional salsa.

Air Fryer Sausages
Servings: 8
Cooking Time: 10 Minutes
Ingredients:
- 8 sausages

Directions:
1. Preheat the air fryer to 180C (350F)
2. Pierce each sausage with a knife or fork.
3. Lay sausages in the air fryer basket.
4. Cook for 10 minutes, checking on them and turning them over after 5 minutes.
Notes
Use any sausages you want to - any flavour and any size. For smaller sausages check on them before 10 minutes as they will cook in a quicker time.

Air Fryer Bratwurst
Servings: 5
Cooking Time: 15 Minutes
Ingredients:
- 1 pound uncooked bratwurst
- 5 hoagie rolls optional
- toppings for serving dijon mustard, sauerkraut, pickles, etc

Directions:
1. Preheat the air fryer to 360°F.
2. Place the brats in a single layer in the air fryer basket.
3. Cook them for 8 minutes, then flip and cook for an additional 5-6 minutes or until they reach an internal temperature of 165°F.
4. Serve in rolls and/or with desired toppings.
Notes
Ensure brats reach an internal temperature of 165°F.
Do not pierce the brats before cooking or they will lose their juices. Use caution when checking the temperature, they can squirt hot liquid when pierced.
Allow brats to cool for a few minutes before serving or topping.

Air Fryer Taco Calzones

Servings: 4
Cooking Time: 10 Minutes

Ingredients:
- 1 tube Pillsbury thin crust pizza dough
- 1 cup taco meat
- 1 cup shredded cheddar

Directions:
1. Spread out your sheet of pizza dough on a clean surface. Using a pizza cutter, cut the dough into 4 even squares.
2. Cut each square into a large circle using the pizza cutter. Set the dough scraps aside to make cinnamon sugar bites.
3. Top one half of each circle of dough with 1/4 cup taco meat and 1/4 cup shredded cheese.
4. Fold the empty half over the meat and cheese and press the edges of the dough together with a fork to seal it tightly. Repeat with all four calzones.
5. Gently pick up each calzone and spray it with pan spray or olive oil. Arrange them in your Air Fryer basket.
6. Cook the calzones at 325° for 8-10 minutes. Watch them closely at the 8 minute mark so you don't overcook them.
7. Serve with salsa and sour cream.
8. To make cinnamon sugar bites, cut the scraps of dough into even sized pieces, about 2 inches long. Add them to the Air Fryer basket and cook at 325° for 5 minutes. Immediately toss with 1:4 cinnamon sugar mixture.

Buttermilk Ranch Dressing

Servings: 16

Ingredients:
- 1 cup buttermilk
- ⅔ cup mayonnaise (I use low fat)
- ⅔ cup sour cream (I use low fat)
- 1 tablespoon fresh chives chopped
- 1 tablespoon fresh dill chopped
- 1 tablespoon fresh parsley chopped
- ¾ teaspoon garlic powder
- ¾ teaspoon onion powder
- ½ teaspoon salt & pepper (each)

Directions:
1. Mix all ingredients in a bowl.
2. Refrigerate at least 30 minutes before serving.

Notes
Reduce buttermilk to ¾ cup to make ranch dip. If using dried herbs, use 1 teaspoon of each (instead of 1 tablespoon).
Keeps 1 week in the fridge.

Air Fryer Reheating Leftover Pizza

Servings: 1
Cooking Time: 6 Minutes

Ingredients:
- 1-2 slices leftover pizza
- oil spray , (optional to lightly coat the pizza so toppings don't dry out - need depends on yoout particular toppings)
- EQUIPMENT
- Air Fryer

Directions:
1. Place foil or perforated parchment sheet to base on air fryer basket, rack or tray. Place the pizza on top. If needed, lightly spray the top of pizza so that the toppings don't burn or dry out (optional).
2. Air Fry at 360°F/180°C for 3-6 minutes or until cooked to your desired crispness. If unsure, start cooking for 3 minutes first. Then check to see if it's to your liking. Cook additional minute or two if you want the pizza to be crispier. Deep dish crusts will take a little longer, while thin crust will be slightly quicker.
3. Let the slice of pizza cool for a touch & enjoy!

NOTES
Air Frying Tips and Notes:
Recipe timing is based on a non-preheated air fryer. If cooking in multiple slices back to back, the following slices may cook a little quicker because the air fryer is already hot.
Recipes were tested in 3.7 to 6 qt. air fryers. If using a larger air fryer, the pizza slices might cook quicker so adjust cooking time.

Air Fryer Spaghetti Squash

Servings: 4
Cooking Time: 35 Minutes

Ingredients:
- 1 medium spaghetti squash about 3 pounds
- 1 tablespoon olive oil
- ½ teaspoon kosher salt
- ¼ teaspoon black pepper

Directions:
1. Preheat the air fryer to 370°F.
2. Cut the spaghetti squash in half lengthwise. Scoop out the seeds and discard (or save for roasting).
3. Brush the cut side of the squash with oil and season with salt & pepper.
4. Place cut side up in the air fryer and cook 25-30 minutes or until tender and the strands separate easily with a fork.
5. Once cooked, run a fork along the strands of the squash to separate.
6. Toss with butter if desired or season with additional salt and pepper.

Notes
Spaghetti squash seeds can be saved and cooked like pumpkin seeds.
Cook time can vary slightly based on the size of the squash.
Once the strands are separated, they can be topped with your favorite meat sauce and placed back into the squash shells. Top them with mozzarella cheese and air fryer until browned and bubbly.
Keep leftovers in the fridge for up to 3 days. Freeze leftovers in zippered bags for up to 6 months. Let thaw at room temperature before using.

Air Fryer Frozen Corn Dogs

Servings: 5
Cooking Time: 10 Minutes

Ingredients:
- 5 frozen corn dogs

Directions:
1. Preheat your air fryer to 350 degrees.
2. Place the frozen corn dogs into the air fryer and cook for 10-13 minutes, checking the inside with an Instant Read Thermometer.
3. Remove the corn dogs from the air fryer and enjoy!

NOTES
HOW TO REHEAT CORN DOGS IN AN AIR FRYER:
Preheat your air fryer to 400 degrees.
Cook the corn dogs in the air fryer for 3-5 minutes, remove them from the air fryer, and enjoy!

Air-fryer White Pizza

Servings: 4
Cooking Time: 6 Minutes

Ingredients:
- 1 recipe Food Processor Pizza Dough
- 2 tablespoon olive oil
- ¾ cup whole milk ricotta cheese
- 1 cup shredded mozzarella cheese (4 oz.)
- 1 teaspoon crushed red pepper
- ½ teaspoon sea salt flakes
- 2 tablespoon chopped fresh basil
- Honey (optional)
- Food Processor Pizza Dough
- Olive oil or nonstick cooking spray
- 2 cup all-purpose flour
- 1 package active dry yeast
- 1 teaspoon sugar
- ½ teaspoon salt
- 1 tablespoon olive oil
- ⅔ cup warm water (105°F to 115°F)

Directions:
1. Preheat air fryer at 375°F. Divide Food Processor Pizza Dough into four 4-oz. portions. On a lightly floured surface, roll one portion of dough into an 8-inch circle. Prick all over with a fork. Place in air-fryer basket and cook 3 minutes. Remove from basket and place, top side down, on work surface.
2. Drizzle crust lightly with 1 1/2 tsp. of the oil and spread with 3 Tbsp. of the ricotta cheese. Sprinkle with 1/4 cup of the mozzarella cheese, 1/4 tsp. of the crushed red pepper, and 1/8 tsp. of the salt. Return

pizza to air-fryer basket and cook 3 to 4 minutes or until cheese is melted and golden. Repeat with remaining dough and toppings.

3. Before serving, sprinkle pizzas with basil and, if desired, drizzle with honey.
4. Food Processor Pizza Dough
5. Coat a medium bowl with nonstick cooking spray; set aside. In a food processor combine flour, yeast, sugar, and salt. With the food processor running, add olive oil and warm water. Process until a dough forms. Remove and shape into a smooth ball. Place dough in the prepared bowl; turn once to coat dough surface. Cover bowl with plastic wrap. Let stand in a warm place until doubled in size (45 to 60 minutes).

*Tip
For a delicious garlic-herb crust, add 1 Tbsp. dried Italian seasoning, crushed, and 2 cloves garlic, minced, to the flour mixture when preparing the dough.

*Make-Ahead Directions:
At this point, the dough portions can be placed in a storage container that has been lightly coated with nonstick cooking spray or brushed with olive oil. Cover and store in the refrigerator for up to 24 hours. Or place each dough portion in a freezer bag that has been lightly coated with nonstick cooking spray or brushed with olive oil. Seal, label, and freeze up to 3 months. Thaw in the refrigerator before using.

Air Fryer Cacio E Pepe Spaghetti Squash
Servings: 2

Ingredients:
- 1 medium spaghetti squash (about 2 lb.), halved lengthwise
- 2 tbsp. extra-virgin olive oil, plus more for drizzling
- 2 tbsp. grated Parmesan, plus more for serving
- 3/4 tsp. kosher salt
- 1/2 tsp. freshly ground black pepper, plus more
- Torn fresh basil leaves, torn, for serving

Directions:
1. In an air-fryer basket, arrange one-half of squash cut side down. Cook at 360° until squash is tender and golden, 20 to 25 minutes. Repeat with other half of squash.
2. Scrape and fluff insides of squash with a fork and transfer to a medium bowl; reserve shells for serving, if desired. Add oil, Parmesan, salt, and 1/2 teaspoon pepper to bowl and toss to combine.
3. Stuff insides back into reserved shells or divide between plates. Drizzle with more oil. Top with more Parmesan, pepper, and basil.

3 Cheese Air Fryer Mini Pizzas
Cooking Time: 4 Minutes

Ingredients:
- 1 can biscuits
- ⅓ cup pizza sauce
- ⅓ cup mozzarella cheese shredded
- ⅓ cup cheddar cheese shredded
- 2 tablespoon parmesan cheese grated

Directions:
1. Preheat air fryer to 400°F.
2. Roll out the biscuits into flat circles.
3. Top with the pizza sauce and cheese.
4. Place in the air fryer basket and cook for 4 minutes or until cheese is melted.

Air Fried Spicy Duck Leg
Servings: 4

Ingredients:
- 2 duck legs
- For the marinade
- 1 orange, juiced
- 1/2 tsp fresh ginger
- 1 tsp granulated garlic
- 4 tbsp olive oil
- Chilli powder, as much as you like
- Salt and pepper
- COOKING MODE
- When entering cooking mode - We will enable your screen to stay 'always on' to avoid any unnecessary interruptions whilst you cook!

Directions:
1. Combine all marinate ingredients.
2. Coat duck leg everywhere with the marinate and leave in in the fridge, in air tight container for at least 2-4h to marinate.
3. Set ninja health grill on air frying mode, 180 C for 25 min
4. Turn duck leg every 7-10min.
5. Serve with salad and grilled potatoes.

Air Fryer Hot Pockets

Servings: 1
Cooking Time: 12 Minutes

Ingredients:
- 1 Frozen Hot Pocket
- EQUIPMENT
- Air Fryer

Directions:
1. Place the frozen hot pocket in the air fryer basket. If cooking multiple hot pockets, spread out into a single even layer. No oil spray is needed.
2. Air Fry at 380°F/193°C for 10 minutes. If needed, flip the hot pocket over and cook for another 1-3 minutes or until cooked to your preference. Cooking more than 1 hot pocket at a time might require more cooking time.

NOTES

Air Frying Tips and Notes:

No Oil Necessary. Cook Frozen - Do not thaw first.

Shake or turn if needed. Don't overcrowd the air fryer basket.

Recipe timing is based on a non-preheated air fryer. If cooking in multiple batches of hot pockets back to back, the following batches may cook a little quicker.

Recipes were tested in 3.7 to 6 qt. air fryers. If using a larger air fryer, the hot pockets might cook quicker so adjust cooking time.

Printed in Great Britain
by Amazon

30110230R00064